WINNING
BIG
With BARGAIN STOCKS

HOW TO INVEST SUCCESSFULLY IN NEW
ISSUES, WARRANTS, AND STOCKS OF
TURNAROUND COMPANIES UNDER $10

BILL MATHEWS

NEWLY
REVISED!

Dearborn
Financial Publishing, Inc.

While a great deal of care has been taken to provide accurate and current information, the ideas, suggestions, general principles and conclusions presented in this text are subject to local, state and federal laws and regulations, court cases and any revisions of same. The reader is thus urged to consult legal counsel regarding any points of law—this publication should not be used as a substitute for competent legal advice.

Publisher: Kathleen A. Welton
Associate Editor: Karen A. Christensen
Managing Editor: Jack L. Kiburz
Editorial Assistant: Kristen G. Landreth
Cover Design: Salvatore Concialdi

Published by Dearborn Financial Publishing, Inc.

Printed in the United States of America

94 95 96 10 9 8 7 6 5 4 3 2 1

Library of Congress Cataloging-in-Publication Data

Mathews, Bill.
    Winning big with bargain stocks : how to invest successfully in new
issues, warrants, and stocks of turnaround companies under $10 /
Bill Mathews. — Newly rev.
        p. cm.
    Includes index.
    ISBN 0-7931-0948-5
    1. Investments—United States—Handbooks, manuals, etc.
    2. Stocks—United States—Handbooks, manuals, etc.   I. Title.
    HG4921.M35   1994
    332.63′22—dc20   94-17311
                                                          CIP

CONTENTS

Identifying and Selecting a Quality
Turnaround • Turnarounds To Avoid

PREFACE

When I wrote the first edition of *Winning Big with Bargain Stocks,* my statistics indicated that the U.S. economy and the stock market were positioned for rapid growth. I predicted in my newsletter, *The CHEAP Investor,* that smart investors could outpace the Dow by purchasing stock from low-priced, quality small companies.

At that time, the overwhelming majority of Wall Street analysts and the media were bombarding us with a very gloomy forecast. They believed that the huge conglomerates, which were downsizing with a vengeance, indicated that the economy and the market were in trouble. Those analysts missed the fact that the Fortune 100 companies aren't the true job creators in today's economy. While the dinosaurs—IBM, General Motors and DuPont—were drastically cutting back, thousands of small- to mid-size companies were exploding. Despite the much ballyhooed reductions by those conglomerates, over 1.5 million new jobs were created in 1993!

Investors who followed the Wall Street analysts' advice missed out on a tremendous bull market. Since 1991, small stocks have been the biggest winners in the investment arena, easily surpassing the Dow, which rose a good 30 percent. As positive economic indicators continue in early 1994, the analysts and media are attributing the gains to the Clinton administration's policies. They're wrong again. The

Clinton economic plan didn't become effective until January 1994, and as I write this, it's still too early for those policies to greatly impact the economy.

While I normally don't care who is president, as long as he or she does a good job, the current administration has the potential to derail our strong economy. Right now it is more interested in policies that increase government interference and regulation. It has become more important than ever to invest wisely in quality companies that can withstand the economic downturn we could experience if the administration doesn't do more to promote business expansion.

The main goal of *Winning Big with Bargain Stocks* is to help you become the *best* investor you can be. Statistics indicate that 70 percent of all investors lose money in the stock market. Why? Most investors buy poor quality stocks at too high a price and either get greedy and don't take their profit or ignore signals that indicate the price may go down. They then end up selling their stocks for a loss.

This book will give you a better understanding of the stock market in general and how to pick quality stocks, buy them at a good price and sell for a tidy profit. It will explain why you should specialize in one area and how to avoid stock scams.

Winning Big with Bargain Stocks is an expanded version of the college course that I taught and refined for over 15 years. The book is full of practical advice on investing in bargain stocks and contains numerous examples. You can study it leisurely at your own pace to learn the ins and outs of investing in bargain stocks. I'm sure it will be a convenient reference book that you will use again and again.

This book was written in easy-to-understand language in a format that moves from the basics into more specific concepts. It's designed to help you learn the essential information you need to know how to make an educated judgment on the value of an investment.

It also shows you how to test your stock analysis abilities without risking any money. Once you're convinced you have learned how to make wiser investment decisions, you can move on to the excitement of investing your money in stocks that you know have the potential for good profits.

By purchasing this book, you have taken the first step to becoming a better investor. Now make sure that you spend the necessary time to get the most benefit from it. Let *Winning Big with Bargain Stocks* be your guide to following your investment dream to huge profits.

I welcome your comments on the book and hope you find it interesting, educational and most of all, profitable.

Bill Mathews, Editor
The CHEAP Investor
Mathews and Associates, Inc.
2549 W. Golf Road, Suite 350
Hoffman Estates, IL 60194
708-830-5666
708-830-5797 (fax)

CHAPTER

1

Following Your
Investment Dream

Knowledge is power. If an investor is knowledgeable about a stock, he or she can make an educated decision on whether or not to purchase it. The investor will not have to rely on anyone else who may or may not be more interested in a commission than in the quality of the investment. This book will provide you with all the necessary information to analyze a stock on your own, to realize what is a good price to purchase the stock, to recognize when to take your profit and to learn how to protect your profits.

YOUR FIRST STEPS BEFORE CONSIDERING
ANY INVESTMENT

Over 50 million Americans from all walks of life own stock in U.S. businesses. Making money from buying and selling stocks is an exciting proposition; before you begin, however, you must ask yourself if you are ready to invest.

You don't need to earn $100,000 a year to invest. In fact, a 1990 survey by the New York Stock Exchange (NYSE) found that the median household income for investors was $43,800. However, you should take a hard look at your financial situation. Your income should cover your basic expenses, and you should set up an emergency fund equal to six months' salary. Once you have made sure that you are financially secure, your remaining funds can be invested. *Any* investment involves some degree of risk, so the funds you have earmarked should be money that you can afford to lose.

After you have decided to invest your extra cash, analyze just what you want to accomplish through the investments. Your individual situation should guide you. If you are near retirement or already living on a fixed income, most of your investing program should be designed to earn dividends or interest while protecting your principal. However, you should invest a small percentage in common stocks so you can participate in the growth of our economic system.

If you receive more income from various sources or are young enough that you believe you can take more risks with your capital, investing a larger percentage in quality, low-priced stocks can be your ticket to high profits. You can place part of your capital in a program with a lower, but more secure, return and then invest the balance in quality bargain (or CHEAP) stocks with a greater profit potential.

THE CHEAP PHILOSOPHY APPROACH TO INVESTING

I originally developed the CHEAP philosophy in response to my personal investment experiences. After 15 years of teaching college-level investment courses, I have tested, modified and perfected this philosophy. It has become the cornerstone of my newsletter, *The CHEAP Investor*, which tens of thousands of investors across the country have successfully used since 1981.

My introduction to investing occurred during the late 1960s, when my broker recommended buying AT&T because he thought it was the highest-quality blue chip stock available and would therefore be my best investment. At that time AT&T was the most profitable company in the country, and its stock was selling at $63 per share. As an avid admirer of the automobile industry, I also became interested in American Motors (since bought by Chrysler), which was producing several very innovative and exciting cars. When I called my broker to buy some American Motors stock, he tried to persuade me to give up the foolish notion, claiming that the company was on the verge of bankruptcy as it had just set a new record for the largest loss suffered by any company.

When my broker realized that he couldn't talk me out of my "crazy" idea, he asked me to sign a statement indicating that he had not recommended buying the $3 stock. I signed the statement and he bought the stock. While I invested the same amount of money in

American Motors that I did in AT&T, because it was only $3 compared to $63, I received 21 times as many shares of American Motors stock.

Six months later AT&T dropped from $63 to $48 or –24 percent, but American Motors rose from $3 to $13 or +333 percent! It didn't matter that AT&T was the most profitable and recognized blue chip and that American Motors had experienced the largest loss in history. I learned a valuable lesson, one that changed my life forever. From that point on, I always questioned investing in a company just because it was a blue chip company. Although I didn't know what a turnaround stock was when I invested in American Motors, I soon learned.

Another episode changed my view of investing. A neighbor of mine worked for S.S. Kresge, and one day he was complaining to me that he had an option but no money to buy 11 shares of the stock at $33 per share (a 20 percent discount on its market price). I had some extra money, so I offered him 10 percent of the profits if he let me bankroll the option to buy those 11 shares for $363. Over the next year, S.S. Kresge's stock moved up to $99 and split three for one, giving us 33 shares at $33 each. Over the next two years, it again reached $99 and split three for one. Now we had 99 shares at $33 or $3,267. The stock continued to move upward, and a few years later we sold out at $62 for $6,138. In a little more than five years, we had parlayed a $363 investment to more than $6,000!

Why did the stock soar? While you may not recognize the name S.S. Kresge, you probably recognize its creation, K mart, which changed the retailing industry. When I originally bought the stock, the company had produced tremendous increases in sales and earnings, and its stock moved up accordingly. During that same time period Sears, the world's largest retailer, experienced only a slight increase in its stock price. I learned that I was wiser to invest in a smaller company with good growth potential than in a mature industry leader.

As I continued to develop my investment philosophy, I realized that I achieved much of my success by acting contrary to the recommendations of Wall Street and the media. In essence, I became a successful investor not by following the crowd but by challenging it. These experiences, along with my teaching and research, formed the foundation of the CHEAP philosophy. The 12 rules that constitute the CHEAP philosophy are as follows:

1. *Become an educated investor.* Let's face it, no one has as much interest as you do in seeing your money grow. Your best investment is to spend the time educating yourself about the investing

process so you can make intelligent investment decisions. You don't buy a house without checking it out. Why buy a stock when you know nothing about the company? Becoming an educated investor will not only save you money in commissions; it should greatly increase your investing success.

2. *Invest in a company, not in a market.* The market is only one factor that determines whether a stock's price will go up or down. The major factor affecting the direction a company's stock will move is the quality of the company itself. If the company has increased its sales and earnings, the stock usually will move upward regardless of the market. However, if the company has experienced huge losses and decreased sales, its stock price normally will drop even if the market is moving upward.

3. *Don't be a jack-of-all-trades and a master of none—specialize in one specific area.* Learning everything about all types of investments is overwhelming. A way to reduce this to a more manageable load is to specialize in one area of investing. Becoming an educated investor in a specific area can prove extremely lucrative. My research shows that investorsn specializing in quality, low-priced stocks can far outpace the market.

4. Don't fall victim to the greed/fear trap. A pitfall that catches most investors at one time or another is the greed/fear trap. Greed enters into the picture when an investor has made a nice profit on a stock but hesitates to take the profit because the investor believes he or she can get even more. When the stock price starts to fall, the investor becomes afraid to sell because he or she assumes it will go up again and watches as the stock moves back down to or below the original purchase price.

5. Don't lose money by investing in the wrong priced stocks. When investors purchase higher-priced stocks, they encounter two obstacles to successful investing. The first is that they can't afford to buy as many shares, so commission fees can wipe out a major portion of the profit. The second is that many higher-priced stocks are so expensive that it is almost mathematically impossible for them to double in price. They have already experienced their major growth.

6. *To make profits, carefully consider the number of shares you control.* Commissions for 1,000 shares of stock may cost only two or three times the price for 100 shares. This can directly affect your profit. In addition, if you buy 100 shares of a $30 stock and 1,000 shares of a $3 stock and both go up $1, the $30 stock will realize a $100 profit, while the $3 stock will experience a $1,000 profit.

7. *Always look at profits and losses in percentages, not in points.* How would you have profited if the $30 stock went up $5 and the $3 stock rose only $1? Offhand, you may say the $30 stock performed better. However, if you actually figure out the profit percentage, you would see that the $30 stock moved up 16.7 percent while the $3 stock rose 33.3 percent!

8. *Consider the purchase price of a stock to determine your profit.* Most stocks are cyclical. This means that they move up near their 52-week high, then down near the 52-week low and then back up again. If you buy a stock near its 52-week high, the law of averages is against you. It is much smarter to buy a quality stock near its 52-week low, where it has greater profit potential.

9. *Being patient can pay off in profits.* It takes patience to wait for a stock to dip near its 52-week low price, but this can mean the difference between a profit and a loss. Many times I have followed a stock for a year or more before it achieved the perfect combination of being a high-quality company at a low price.

10. *Buy your stock when no one wants it, and sell it when everyone wants to buy.* If you invest contrary to the masses, you will be able to buy the stock while there is little demand for it and the price is low. Likewise, when other investors are clamoring to buy the stock and its price goes up, you already have made a nice profit and can sell while others are buying at a much higher price.

11. *Don't take anyone else's word; investigate before you invest.* Many times an investor is so blinded by greed that he or she forgets to ask any questions about the investment. Letting someone else make your investment decisions certainly is easier, yet it makes you more susceptible to high-pressure scam artists. Telephone scam artists pressure you to buy right away without thinking it over. Never buy any investment without getting information *in writing* so that you can analyze it. Doing so can save a lot of money and trouble.

12. *Follow your stock price so you don't miss major profit opportunities.* Many investors become lazy after they have purchased a stock and don't follow its price. That can be their downfall. Some stocks are very volatile and may double in price only to fall back a week or two later. If the investor hasn't been watching the price, he or she may miss a great opportunity for profit.

Perhaps the biggest eye opener for me was discovering that I could make more profitable investments by choosing stocks myself rather than relying on a broker. To maintain my success, I realized that I had to learn as much as possible about the stock to intelligently decide whether or not it was a good investment.

☐   **RULE 1**   ☐

Become an educated investor.

Whenever your broker, friend or relative gives you a stock tip, don't immediately buy the stock without checking. Stop to think for a moment. Take the time to find out what the current stock price is. Is it near the stock's 52-week high or low price? The cardinal rule of investing is to buy a stock at a low price and sell it for a higher price. If the stock you are interested in is already at its historical high, your chances of making a profit are greatly reduced, so stay away from it. If the stock is near its 52-week low price, this is a great starting point. However, you must take the next step, which is to call the company for a full investment packet and use that information to analyze its profit potential.

Why do reasonable people who would never consider buying a car without checking to see if it is a good purchase blindly invest thousands of dollars in companies that basically have nothing to offer? I believe that most investors are intimidated by the overwhelming number of companies and types of investments. They figure that they can never learn enough about these companies and investments and thus must rely on experts. This is okay as long as the expert knows what he or she is doing. But if the expert doesn't, the investor usually finds out only after he or she is several thousand dollars poorer.

WELCOME TO THE WORLD OF BARGAIN INVESTMENTS

The stock market can be mystifying to the novice. For example, just what does it mean when someone says a stock is at $11\frac{1}{8}$? Even though the stock price is sometimes referred to as points, it is translated into dollars, so that $11\frac{1}{8}$ is actually 11 and $\frac{1}{8}$ dollars or $11.125. Why does the stock market use fractions such as $\frac{1}{8}$ or $\frac{1}{16}$ when our currency is based on tens? I believe that when the original stock market began during the 1700s, it was based on Spanish currency (remember pieces of eight?), and the exchange adopted that breakdown of the dollar. It

Figure 1.1   Conversion of Fractions to Cents

Fraction	Cents	Fraction	Cents	Fraction	Cents	Fraction	Cents
$\frac{1}{32}$	$ .03125	$\frac{9}{32}$	$ .28125	$\frac{17}{32}$	$ .53125	$\frac{25}{32}$	$.78125
$\frac{1}{16}$	.0625	$\frac{5}{16}$	.3125	$\frac{9}{16}$	.5625	$\frac{13}{16}$	.8125
$\frac{3}{32}$	.09375	$\frac{11}{32}$	.34375	$\frac{19}{32}$	.59375	$\frac{27}{32}$	.84375
$\frac{1}{8}$	.125	$\frac{3}{8}$	.375	$\frac{5}{8}$	.625	$\frac{7}{8}$	.875
$\frac{5}{32}$	.15625	$\frac{13}{32}$	.40625	$\frac{21}{32}$	.65625	$\frac{29}{32}$	.90625
$\frac{3}{16}$	.1875	$\frac{7}{16}$	.4375	$\frac{11}{16}$	.6875	$\frac{15}{16}$	.9375
$\frac{7}{32}$	.21875	$\frac{15}{32}$	.46875	$\frac{23}{32}$	.71875	$\frac{31}{32}$	.96875
$\frac{1}{4}$	.25	$\frac{1}{2}$	.50	$\frac{3}{4}$	.75	1	1.00

is outdated, but don't hold your breath waiting for it to be changed. Instead, use Figure 1.1 to convert the fractions into cents.

One of the basics of investing is following the company's stock price. Some stocks don't move very much, and you may need to check them only once a week. However, it is a good idea to follow most stocks daily. Sometimes fantastic news can cause a stock to rise or fall quickly in price, and if you aren't watching, you may miss a profit opportunity.

You can call your broker every day; yet it would be more courteous to check the stock price in *The Wall Street Journal, Investor's Business Daily* or your local newspaper. Figure 1.2 shows the various column headings and what they mean.

The stock table for the Nasdaq (National Association of Securities Dealers Automated Quotations system) market is very similar to the listing in Figure 1.2, except that Nasdaq stocks have a bid and asked price that may be listed. The bid price is what the shareholder would receive if he or she sold the stock, and the asked price is what the shareholder would pay to buy the stock.

HOW INDIVIDUALS CAN EASILY OUTPACE THE MARKET

As you are looking for a stock to invest in, remember that your main concern is whether the company is a good investment, not if the market will go up or down.

Whenever you read about the market going up or down, have you wondered what this actually refers to? Does it mean that every stock on that particular market went up or down? Is it an average? These are good questions to keep in mind the next time you hear a newsper-

son on television solemnly reading, "The market is down 14 points."
In most cases, the newsperson is referring to the Dow Jones Industrial
Average (DJIA), which is an index comprised of 30 stocks. While these
30 stocks may have averaged an upward or downward movement, the
stocks you have invested in could possibly have remained unchanged
or moved in the opposite direction.

☐   **RULE 2**   ☐

Invest in a company, not in a market.

Many investors place too much emphasis on what the market is
doing rather than on whether the company possesses good profit
potential. I strongly believe that a low-priced, quality stock has a good
potential to make profits no matter what the market does. Market
crashes such as the one in 1987 greatly affected the blue chip stocks
and caused panic that in turn affected the majority of lower-priced
stocks. However, the crash didn't cause those quality low-priced
companies to go out of business, and in most cases their stock prices
quickly rebounded.

From the middle of 1981 through most of 1987, the market kept
moving higher and higher. During that time IBM moved from $70 to
a high of $175.88. Buying that stock and holding on to it would have
resulted in a nice profit of 151 percent. However, I have found that a
great number of stocks are cyclical. This means that their stock price
goes up, comes down, goes up again, etc. By purchasing a quality stock
that is near its 52-week low and selling it when the stock gets near its
52-week high, your profit potential is greatly multiplied.

Figure 1.3 shows the price cycle of Fonar Corporation. It displays
the first four buy recommendations that I gave on the stock since
October 1981. The lower figure is the price at which I recommended
Fonar, and the higher figure shows the highest price the stock hit after
my recommendation. Buying and selling this stock obviously would
have given an investor some very nice profits. Because there is no way
of knowing exactly what low and high price a stock will hit, it is best
to buy near the low and sell when the stock price starts to back off
from the high.

Figure 1.2   Typical Newspaper Listing for a Stock on the NYSE and AMEX

52-WEEK HIGH LOW		STOCKS	STOCK SYM.	DIV.	YLD. %	P/E RATIO	SALES 100s	HIGH	LOW	CLOSE	NET CHANGE
8½	3½	BAIRNCO	BZ	.20	5	6	600	4⅝	3⅞	4	+¼
(A)		(B)	(C)	(D)	(E)	(F)	(G)	(H)	(I)	(J)	(K)

(A) *52-Week high/low* — This is the highest and lowest price per share (high is $8.50 per share, low is $3.50 per share) that this stock has traded for during the past 52 weeks.

(B) *Stocks* — This refers to the name of the stock. In this case it is Bairnco Corporation.

(C) *Stock symbol* — This is the group of letters assigned to a stock so that a broker can access the stock on his or her computer to check the price and other information.

(D) *Div.* — The annual cash dividend paid on the stock. Bairnco paid $.20 per share.

(E) *Yld.(%)* — The dividend in terms of yield percent. Because there is a $.20 dividend and the close of the stock is $4, the yield percent is 5.

(F) *P/E ratio* — The price-earnings (P/E) ratio for this stock is 6. The previous day's closing price divided by the latest 12-month per share earnings for the company becomes the P/E ratio. This is used to measure comparative values among different stocks. If there is no P/E ratio, the company is not making money; if there is a P/E ratio, the company is profitable.

(G) *Sales (100s)* — Refers to the day's trading volume of this stock. The number 600 is in hundreds of shares. Therefore, a total of 60,000 shares was traded that day. (You must have both a buy and a sell transaction to constitute a trade.)

(H) *High* — This is the highest price ($4.625 per share) at which the stock was traded during the day.

(I) *Low* — This is the lowest price ($3.875 per share) at which the stock was traded during the day.

(J) *Close* — When the stock exchange bell rings and the market is closed, the last or *closing* price ($4 per share) for which the stock was traded.

(K) *Net change* — The change in the closing price from the previous day's closing price. In this example, Bairnco was up ¼ or $.25 per share when compared to the previous day's closing price.

**Figure 1.3   Price Cycle of Fonar Corporation—First Four Buy
Recommendations after Going Public**

For example, an investor spent $1,000 to buy 200 shares of Fonar at the originally recommended new-issue price of $5 and watched the stock rise to $12.50. When the stock price started to back off, he sold it at $10 and doubled his money to $2,000. If he continued to follow the stock and bought into it again at $5 the next time, he could purchase 400 shares with his $2,000. Once the stock started falling from the $15.50 high, even if he sold the stock for $12.50, the investor would have increased that initial $1,000 investment to $5,000.

By the way, if the investor had bought Fonar at the $5 new-issue price when I first recommended it and had just held on to it, he wouldn't be very happy right now since the stock is currently at $3, or down 40 percent. However, Fonar has tripled from my recent buy recommendation at $1.15.

For the past several years many stocks have experienced smaller and more frequent price swings. In this type of market, if you have a stock that has risen 30, 40 or 50 percent, you should consider taking your profit before the price moves down again and you have lost the opportunity. As you can see, a good method for making money in this volatile market is to trade quality, low-priced cyclical stocks.

What should you do if you have sold your cyclical stock for a profit and it continues to rise? You don't buy that stock at the much higher price, hoping it will continue to go higher; this is a great way to lose money. Ideally, you should follow several cyclical investment candidates. Then you can invest your capital in one of the other stocks if it is at a good low price.

This chapter has given you some background to prepare you to master investing in bargain stocks. In Chapter 2 you will learn why common stocks are your best investment and why so many foreign investors buy U.S. stocks. Chapter 3 will teach you how the various exchanges work, how you buy or sell on the exchanges and why the Dow Jones Industrials Average may be very misleading. Chapter 4 explains why companies sell stock and how you can become a better investor by specializing in one area. Chapter 5 shows you how to easily and profitably analyze stocks. Chapter 6 explains how the small investor can outpace the institutions by investing in stocks under $10.

Chapter 7 details the new-issue process and explains how to easily read a prospectus. Chapter 8 explains why companies go into bankruptcy and how you can profit from buying them when they are undervalued. Chapter 9 will show you how to make huge profits on turnaround stocks. Chapter 10 explains warrants and how to buy them wisely. Chapter 11 illustrates the difference between discount and full-service brokerage firms and helps you locate the best broker for your needs. Chapter 12 shows you how to buy stocks at the best price. Chapter 13 offers tips for selling for the best profits.

Chapter 14 teaches how economics can affect the stock market. Chapter 15 explains how you can profit from plummeting stock prices caused by major incidents such as the Middle East oil crisis or the 1987 stock market crash. Chapter 16 teaches you how to be a scam-proof investor. Chapter 17 explains how you can apply what you have learned in simulated trading. Chapter 18 tests what you have learned. Also included is a glossary containing many of the important terms used by the investment industry.

So study this book to learn how you can best take advantage of bargain stocks.

CHAPTER

2

Why You Should Invest in Common Stocks

At the end of the 1980s Japan was number one in the amount of cash savings per individual, with an average of $40,000. The United States ranked number 11, with just $10,000 savings per individual. Many people were surprised by these statistics and wondered how the Japanese had been able to build their savings so quickly. While several factors entered into it, a big reason why they greatly increased their savings was their investments in *common stock*. The Japanese invest as individuals and through their institutions, banks and pension funds. Americans, on the other hand, missed out on a great investment opportunity after the 1987 stock market crash. After the crash small investors and institutions moved away from buying common stocks that create new jobs and instead invested in options, futures, certificates of deposit (CDs), junk bonds and other investments that do little to build economic growth. However, the courageous investors who recognized a bargain and invested when no one else wanted those severely undervalued quality stocks saw their assets increase dramatically.

Any individual can participate in our free enterprise system by starting a company and becoming a direct owner. However, because most people don't have the necessary capital or entrepreneurial skills, they can indirectly share in the growth and prosperity of a company by investing in its common stock. An investor with a small amount of money can become a partial owner of a growing corporation and enjoy many of the same benefits as the entrepreneur.

This opportunity is available to everyone in our economic system. No wonder that more and more people are taking advantage of it and investing in common stocks. Since interest rates have plunged the past two years, more investors are buying common stocks to obtain a higher rate of return. This chapter will help you understand what common stocks are and why you should invest in them.

Many foreign investors choose to buy U.S. common stocks instead of their own countries' stocks. Why? The United States is unique. Our political stability and the strength of our economy are unmatched, and foreign investors are flocking to purchase U.S. common stocks because of their safety and tremendous growth potential. The bottom line is that foreign investors can receive a better return from U.S. stocks.

Even if you have never called a broker and bought a common stock, you already may be investing in them through your pension fund, profit-sharing plan, mutual fund or other investment that you own. The major attraction of common stocks is that, over the long run, they outperform almost all other investments. They are easy to buy and sell, fairly simple to research and, most important of all, volatile with the potential for producing excellent profits.

WHAT IS A COMMON STOCK?

When you purchase common stock, you become a part owner of the company. The number of shares you buy determines your percentage of ownership in the firm. As a common-stock owner, you can share in the future of the company's earnings as well as vote (one vote per share) to decide on major issues affecting the company, such as a merger. The ownership of common stock gives the investor a way of participating in the growth of virtually any corporation. In addition, owning common stock helps protect the investor against inflation, for over the years common stocks have far outpaced inflation.

Because thousands of companies offer shares of common stock, the investor has the opportunity to invest in a broad spectrum of industries. With virtually any investment, you face some risk of losing part or all of the investment. However, by investing in quality, low-priced stocks, the investor can greatly reduce the risk and increase the profit potential.

There basically are two ways to make money from common stock: (1) from dividends or (2) from appreciation (from the sale of the stock after it increases from your purchase price). A stock pays dividends only when it is profitable. However, a stock's price can go up for many reasons. The stock price should move upward when any of the following occur:

- The company has increased its sales and profits.
- The company's industry is experiencing a boom period that may favorably affect the stock's price.
- The company has announced a new product, acquisition or large sales contract.
- The company is approached for a merger or takeover (or there are rumors that this will be attempted).
- A major Wall Street brokerage firm recommends buying the stock.

Of course, sometimes the company can announce tremendous news, and the stock price stays the same or goes down. Likewise, the company can experience poor earnings or bad management or announce negative news, and the stock price goes up. The stock price reaction is not always rational.

TYPES OF COMMON STOCKS

The term *common stock* is actually a generic name for several different categories of stocks. Sometimes a stock may fall into more than one category; for example, a company may be considered both a blue chip and an income stock.

Blue Chip Stocks

These are widely known companies with long histories of earnings and dividends. Wall Street promotes blue chips as long-term, "safe" investments that presumably offer a low-risk potential and provide a modest return. IBM, General Motors, General Electric and the other well-known stocks listed on the Dow Jones indexes are considered blue chip stocks.

The problem with blue chip stocks is that they typically are extremely high priced ($60 and up), and the small investor can purchase only a few shares. Blue chips are huge, established companies that have already experienced a major period of growth. In my opinion they offer the investor a small return on an overpriced stock. Blue chip stocks are generally listed on the New York Stock Exchange (NYSE), and most of the time they follow the market on its upward and downward swings. However, because their stock prices are so high, these blue chip stocks usually do not move up over 100 percent in a year.

Growth Stocks

Although they are less well known than blue chips, growth stocks still receive a good amount of publicity. They have enjoyed a history of increasing sales and earnings for several years and are promoted by Wall Street as good investments in a bull market. Because they are younger (10 to 25 years old) and smaller than the blue chip companies, they offer greater growth potential and usually grow faster than the economy and other companies in their industry. If a growth stock gives any dividend, it is very small. Motorola, AST Research, Wal-Mart, Arrow Electronics and Intel are examples of growth companies.

Growth stocks normally range in price from $20 to $55, which means that the small investor again can afford only a few shares. The stocks tend to be extremely volatile. They usually grow at higher percentages than blue chip stocks, but they rely heavily on the health of the economy and their industry for that growth.

Income Stocks

These well-established companies have existed for a long time. They experience very small growth, normally about the same as the gross domestic product (GDP), formerly known as the gross national product. However, the company returns most of its profits to the shareholder in the form of dividends. Income stocks tend to be high priced, and Wall Street sells them as very "safe" investments. In many cases the investor receives a dividend that barely covers inflation. AT&T, Commonwealth Edison and other utility stocks are regarded as income stocks and are not suited to an investor looking for growth.

Fad Stocks

These are usually created by Wall Street analysts in an industry that expands at a much greater rate than the GDP. A fad stock's price typically flies upward as investors jump on the bandwagon to buy. Because its price moves up so fast, the fad stock comes to the attention of more and more investors, and they buy at higher and higher prices. Unfortunately, the fad stock's price quickly becomes extremely over-inflated when compared to the company's true worth.

Many investors lose money in fad stocks because they buy the stock when it is receiving a lot of publicity and the stock price is already high. Common sense eventually prevails, and the stock's price starts to fall (usually after the small investor has just bought it at record high prices). If the investor does not sell quickly, he or she may end up with a stock at a much lower and more reasonable price.

Companies in the high-technology medical industry are prone to fads, especially companies researching cures for major diseases such as cancer or AIDS. Even the rumor that a company may have treatments for such life-threatening diseases can cause a stock to skyrocket.

However, the investors who make truly great profits bought when the stock was low, before it became a fad. They didn't follow the crowd that bought the stock at higher and higher prices. Instead, they sold for tremendous profits when everyone else was buying and driving up the price.

Another hot area is the high-technology entertainment field. We recommended Atari, a computer game company on the American Stock Exchange (AMEX), three times at the $1 level in 1992 and 1993. In late 1993 Atari shot up to $12.75 because of a new game line it planned to introduce.

Cyclical Stocks

These stocks move up and down in a price cycle. Almost all stocks experience a price cycle to some degree. Blue chips and income stocks may not show a great variation from the low to the high price, while some quality, low-priced stocks may experience huge price swings one or more times a year. Properly analyzing a stock to determine its quality and taking advantage of its price cycles can create high profits for the investor.

Low-Priced Stocks

For my purposes, low-priced stocks refer to stocks costing under $10 per share. There are several kinds of low-priced stocks—from highly speculative *penny stocks* (stocks selling for less than $1 per share with little assets, sales or earnings) to the other extreme, quality, low-priced stocks (or as I call them, CHEAP stocks). A *CHEAP stock* is a company with good sales and earnings that is near its 52-week low price. Statistics have proven that quality, low-priced stocks possess great investment potential; thus, this book will concentrate on CHEAP stocks.

COMMON STOCKS OFFER EXCELLENT LIQUIDITY

What is liquidity? *Liquidity* is the ability to convert assets into cash during a short period of time. This should be a major consideration in any investment you make. Anyone who has sold a home is familiar with liquidity. In the late eighties and early nineties, it was not uncommon for months or, in extreme cases, for years to pass between the time a house was offered for sale and actually was sold. While the house price can be determined by professional appraisers, in the end a house is worth only what someone else is willing to pay for it. Most of the time this is lower than the appraised value.

Investors in collectibles such as coins, stamps, collectors' plates, etc., often find that when they want to sell, the market is small, and even though a plate, coin or other collectible may be worth a certain amount according to magazine articles, no one offers anything close to that amount.

During the mid-1980s a friend of mine decided to invest in the new craze—collectors' plates. He excitedly read about the amazing profits he could make. One company claimed the distinction of being a collectors' plate exchange and compared itself with a stock exchange. Supposedly, you could buy plates from the company, and when the price went up, you could sell your plate on the exchange. This sounded like a good opportunity.

My friend decided to invest. A Norman Rockwell plate appreciated from my friend's $17 purchase price to a value of $160 according to literature he received from the exchange. He had purchased ten plates, so he figured his $170 investment was now worth $1,600 for a 841 percent profit in just two years! When he called the exchange to sell his plates, they confirmed the $160 value but recommended that he discount it by 25 percent so the plate would sell faster. There also was a 20 percent commission when the exchange sold his plates. That would net him $96 per plate. This was quite a bit below the $160 value but still not bad. However, after several months the plates hadn't sold, and when he called the exchange, they suggested he again lower his price. He did—to $75, then to $50 and finally to $35. In desperation, he visited stores that sold collectors' plates and finally was able to sell six for $192 or $32 each. He never did sell any plates through the exchange. He now keeps one plate hanging above his desk to remind him of that investment. Since then he has invested only in common stocks because he knows that they offer more liquidity and that it will be easier to find a buyer when he wants to sell.

Common stocks that are traded on the NYSE, the AMEX or the Nasdaq National Market System can quickly be bought or sold for specifically quoted prices. You can call your broker, ask for the latest trade price for the stock and then instruct him or her to buy or sell either for a specific price or at the market price (i.e., the best price available at the time the order is executed). In most cases the computerization of the exchanges allows your broker to buy or sell your stock at the market price in a matter of minutes. The great liquidity of common stocks, compared with many other long-term investments, is a tremendous advantage.

COMMON STOCKS POSSESS GREAT PROFIT POTENTIAL

Numerous types of investments are available. To mention a few, you can buy real estate, rare coins, diamonds, stamps, gold, silver and other precious metals, rare books, futures, commodities, tax shelters, art and options.

Many investors have tried one or more of these investments with varying degrees of success. In fact, after the 1987 crash most investors became disillusioned with common stocks, for they believed that stocks were too speculative. They decided to put their money in "safer" investments, such as options, commodities or futures.

Because they knew nothing about these investments, some became easy marks for scam artists. Others lost money because they weren't knowledgeable enough to make wise investment decisions. They discovered that the people who really make good profits investing in art, coins, diamonds and other collectibles are experts who are educated and who specialize in a specific collectible.

I see more and more investors who turned to other types of investments after the 1987 crash now returning to common stocks poorer but wiser. Over the long term investments in common stocks have generally grown well ahead of the inflation rate. In the 40-year period between 1947 and 1987, the S&P 500 index's annual growth exceeded 12 percent, while inflation has averaged under 4.5 percent.* In general, common stocks not only have kept up with inflation; they have produced an additional 7 percent profit for the investors. While a 7 percent profit may not seem like much, over the years it can really add up. (See Figure 2.1.)

Don't forget that these amounts are for growth *above* the inflation rate. This is real purchasing power, which makes quite a difference. Of course, the 7 percent growth rate is only an average over a long period of time. Year-to-year fluctuations and poor investment choices can adversely affect that rate. On the other hand, making educated decisions to buy CHEAP stocks with real investment potential can result in a much higher rate of return.

Common stocks are an investment for all times. They represent the *best* investment for the vast majority of individuals. They are attractive because over the long haul, common stocks produce better results than most other investments. They have a ready marketplace for both buying and selling. Common stocks are more appropriate and more affordable for the small investor, who may not have much money to invest.

Of course, to make intelligent investment decisions, the investor must be willing to spend some time and effort learning about common stocks. Successful investing in common stocks involves using that knowledge when researching potential investments to determine which stock is the best for your particular goals. This is time well spent and can reap profitable rewards in the near future.

RISK VERSUS PROFIT POTENTIAL

When you invest, avoid ridiculous risks that will only help you lose money. Don't make an investment without any risk at all, for the investment may be so stable that nothing much will happen to it

---

* *NYSE 1992 Fact Book*, New York Stock Exchange, April 1993.

Figure 2.1   7 Percent Growth for $1,000

After	Amount
1 year	$ 1,070
5 years	1,403
10 years	1,967
20 years	3,870
30 years	7,612
40 years	14,974

(including price increases). You must find a happy medium. One way to reduce your risk factor is to *diversify,* that is, to invest in more than one stock.

When you contemplate any type of investment, consider your risk versus your profit potential. Figure 2.2 shows several types of investments and their risk versus profit potential.

Ironically, because the small investor does not have much money to invest, he or she must make the best profit possible. A large investor who has $100,000 can afford to invest in U.S. securities, such as 30-year Treasury bonds at 6 percent. However, a small investor with only $1,000 or $2,000 in capital needs a higher profit rate, or his or her money may never amount to much.

Common stocks offer a high profit potential. However, they also present a greater risk factor. By becoming an educated investor and understanding how the common stock market works, analyzing a stock with good potential, purchasing it at the best price and watching for signs indicating that you should take your profit and sell, you can greatly reduce these risks. The majority of the time, if you invest in a high-quality, low-priced stock, your chances of making a profit are excellent.

COMMON STOCKS AND YOUR TAXES

Each time you buy or sell a stock your brokerage firm will send a confirmation of the trade that details the price you paid or received for your shares, the number of shares traded and the commission. The brokerage firm will also send a copy of the confirmation to the

Figure 2.2 Risk versus Profit Potential

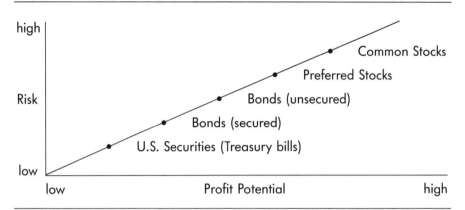

Internal Revenue Service (IRS). *Make sure that you keep all your confirmation forms.* You will need them when you file your taxes.

Note: When listing your stock transactions on tax form Schedule D, remember to subtract your commissions. They are not a part of your profits. Also, check with your tax adviser about whether you can deduct the cost of this book and any financial newsletters and newspapers to which you subscribe.

Capital Gains

Before the 1986 tax revisions, taxpayers could claim both long-term and short-term capital gains. Short-term capital gains were treated as regular income, and the percentage of tax owed was determined by the person's income-tax bracket, which could go up to 50 percent. Long-term capital gains rules applied to stocks held at least six months before they were sold, and the highest tax percentage was 20 percent. Unfortunately, this was changed, and now all stock profits are considered taxable income; the investor pays taxes according to his or her tax bracket up to a capital gains ceiling of 28 percent. (If you sustain many capital losses, you can offset all your gains and up to $3,000 of taxable income every year until you use up all the losses.)

In 1989 and 1990 President Bush pushed to reduce the long-term capital gains tax to a 15 percent maximum. *Long term* in this instance would be defined as being held three years. The Democratic Congress fought against the reduction, claiming it affected only the rich.

However, about 60 million Americans would either be directly or indirectly affected, for many people are involved in pension funds, profit-sharing and life-insurance plans. If such a tax reduction is ever passed, it would be a boon for our economy as well as for the stock market.

By the way, the United States is the *only* industrialized country in the world that even taxes profits from stock investments. Perhaps those foreign investors who buy U.S. stocks have the funds to do so because they don't have to pay capital gains taxes.

USING YOUR STOCK AS COLLATERAL

An advantage of purchasing stocks instead of other investments is that if an emergency arises, you sometimes can use your stock as collateral for a loan. This creates the opportunity to raise money without selling your stock. This is a great advantage if the stock price happens to be at a low point and you would lose money on your investment if you were forced to sell. This alternative allows you to hold the stock until the price is right for selling.

Banks differ, but normally if your stock is listed in *The Wall Street Journal*, your bank can loan you from 50 percent to as much as 80 percent of the value of the stock. Be aware that as long as the stock price continues to rise, there is no problem. However, if your stock price goes down (e.g., by 30 percent), your bank probably will require additional collateral.

CHAPTER

3

How the Stock Exchanges Work

From the visitors' gallery, the floors of the various stock exchanges look like a wild mass of confusion, with people shouting, using strange hand gestures and running back and forth. Believe it or not, that "mass of confusion" is actually very organized and conducts the serious business of buying and selling stocks.

UNDERSTANDING AN EXCHANGE STOCK TRANSACTION

If an investor wants to buy 1,000 shares of M/A-Com at $4.88 per share, she will call her broker, who acts as an intermediary between the client (the buyer) and the seller. For his services, the stockbroker will receive a commission of usually 5 to 10 percent of the stock's cost. The broker transmits the order to his office's trading department, which sends his client's order to his brokerage firm's floor broker on the NYSE. The floor broker is an employee of the brokerage firm who is a member of the exchange. When the floor broker receives the order for 1,000 shares of M/A-Com, he or she will move to the appropriate one out of 22 trading posts on the NYSE floor. There the floor broker will join other floor brokers and the specialist who handles M/A-Com. A typical stock transaction includes the following nine steps:

1. An investor wants to buy 1,000 shares of M/A-Com (MAI) at $4.88.
2. The investor calls a stockbroker.
3. The stockbroker takes the order.
4. The stockbroker transmits the order to the trading department.
5. The trading department passes on the order to the floor broker.
6. The floor broker buys shares from a specialist.
7. The floor broker confirms the purchase to the trading department.
8. The trading department confirms the order to the broker.
9. The stockbroker confirms the completion of the purchase of 1,000 shares of MAI at $4.88 to the client.

At that trading post, M/A-Com's specialist performs his market-making functions, buying and selling the stock. The floor broker will offer $4.88 for 1,000 shares of M/A-Com, which will either be accepted or rejected by the specialist. If the offer is accepted, the floor broker purchases the 1,000 shares either from the specialist's own account or from another floor broker who wants to sell 1,000 shares of M/A-Com through the specialist.

Once he or she has purchased the stock, the floor broker will send a confirmation of the purchase of 1,000 shares of M/A-Com at $4.88 per share to his or her trading department, which in turn contacts the broker, who calls his client to advise her of the completion of the purchase. In many cases, with computerization the whole process takes only a few minutes to complete and confirm.

NEW YORK STOCK EXCHANGE (NYSE)

Founded in 1792, the NYSE is the largest stock exchange in the United States. It is located at 11 Wall Street in New York City and is known as the "Big Board" and the "Exchange." More than 2,000 of the largest, most well-known and profitable U.S. companies are listed on the NYSE.

The NYSE is an unincorporated association headed by a full-time chairperson and governed by a board of directors that represents the public and the exchange membership in about equal proportion. Its functions include membership regulation and surveillance, finance and office services, product development and planning, market servicing and public relations. The NYSE handles legal problems, government regulations and economic research for member firms.

Affiliated corporations include the Depository Trust Company (DTC), a corporation that acts as a go-between for security transfers. Using the DTC reduces the need for physically transferring certificates and cash by recording entries on its computerized system. The DTC debits and credits each member's account for the net assets changing hands. The National Securities Clearing Committee (NSCC) is a committee formed from the consolidation of clearing operations between the NYSE and the AMEX to facilitate the receipt and delivery of security transactions. The Securities Industry Automation Corporation (SIAC) is a subsidiary jointly owned by the NYSE and the AMEX to communicate trade information. Besides sharing information between the two exchanges, the SIAC provides data to other industry quotation services.

The total of 1,366 seats on the NYSE allow the owner to be a member and trade on the floor of the exchange. Brokerage firms own most of these seats. Over 500 member-firm broker/dealers are responsible for maintaining an orderly market in the securities they handle. Most members execute orders for the public, institutions and mutual funds; a few floor traders deal exclusively for their own accounts. Stocks, bonds, warrants, options and rights are traded on the NYSE.

Listing Requirements for the NYSE

To be listed on the NYSE, a company must have

- at least 1.1 million shares of stock publicly held;
- a market value of at least $9 million but no more than $18 million (market value = price per share × number of shares outstanding × an adjustment base currently at 55.06.);
- at least 2,000 shareholders;
- an average pretax income of $2.5 million for the past three years or an aggregate pretax income of $6.5 million for three years with $4.5 million for the most recent year; and
- paid a listing fee, which varies depending on the company's size.

Once a company meets with a listing regional manager, it is asked to send specific information to the exchange, including its past three years of audited balance sheets, Form 10-Ks and annual reports. After reviewing the information, the Listed Company Advisory Committee

(LCAC), which includes chief executive officers (CEOs) and presidents of NYSE member companies, interviews the company. If the LCAC determines that the company meets the requirements, the company is asked to apply formally for listing on the NYSE. This process normally takes six to ten weeks from the date of application to the company's actual listing on the exchange.

Why go through the hassle to become listed? A major advantage of the NYSE listing is the tremendous exposure a company enjoys after joining the 2,000 elite companies already on the exchange. Interestingly, about 90 percent of major institutional investors buy only stocks that are listed on the NYSE. Another advantage is that it is much easier to raise capital once the company is a member of the NYSE.

The NYSE offers a number of publications of interest to the investor. For further information, contact the Publication Department, New York Stock Exchange (11 Wall Street, New York, NY 10005; 212-656-5273).

AMERICAN STOCK EXCHANGE (AMEX)

The AMEX was formed in the 1840s around the time of the California gold rush. It is the second most important stock exchange, although it ranks below the National Association of Securities Dealers Automated Quotations (Nasdaq) system in terms of volume and dollar value of trading. The AMEX was known as the Curb Market from 1911 to 1921 because transactions took place on the curb at Trinity Place in New York City, and sometimes it is still referred to as the "Curb." In 1921 it moved indoors to 86 Trinity Place, where it is still located. In 1929 the name was modified to the New York Curb Exchange. Not until 1953 was its name changed to the American Stock Exchange.

The AMEX operates in a manner similar to the NYSE. It also is an unincorporated association headed by a full-time chairperson and administered by a board of governors. Like the NYSE, the AMEX also trades stocks, bonds, warrants, options and rights. In addition, it trades U.S. Treasuries. More foreign stocks are traded on the AMEX than on any other exchange. Most of the more than 800 stocks listed on the AMEX today are small- to medium-sized businesses with a large concentration of oil, gas and mining companies. Many of the larger and well-known companies (such as Armour, Borden, Dow Chemical,

DuPont, Goodyear, RCA and Standard Oil of California) traded on the AMEX before moving to the NYSE.

Listing Requirements for the AMEX

Normally companies must meet the following minimum standards to qualify for listing on the AMEX. (The membership requirements for the AMEX are significantly lower than those for the NYSE.) A company must have the following:

- at least 500,000 publicly held shares (exclusive of insider holdings);
- a shareholder's equity of $4 million;
- a market value of $3 million (price per share multiplied by the number of shares outstanding);
- a net income of $750,000 for the most recent fiscal year;
- at least 150,000 shares held in lots of 100 to 1,000;
- a minimum stock price of $3 per share (sometimes waived); and
- paid a listing fee.

Perhaps the main reason for a stock to move up from the Nasdaq market to the AMEX is the increased ease in raising capital. When a stock is listed on the Nasdaq market, it must apply individually to each state in which it wants to sell securities. This is very expensive and time consuming. Once the company is listed on the AMEX, it is automatically free to sell its securities in all 50 states.

For more information, contact the American Stock Exchange (86 Trinity Place, New York, NY 10006; 212-306-1000; 800-THE-AMEX or 800-875-1247).

REGIONAL STOCK EXCHANGES

While the term *regional stock exchange* is sometimes used in a derogatory manner, it accurately describes exchange trading located outside of New York. While regional stock exchanges feature the listings of a few local companies, the bulk of their business is obtained from national markets. During the 1960s 14 regional exchanges were in the United States. Since then, the weak have either merged or expired, and only five significant exchanges remain: the Chicago, Pacific, Philadelphia, Boston and Cincinnati stock exchanges.

Trading on these exchanges (except for Cincinnati) is pretty much as I previously described. Stocks with certain local following may be listed exclusively with that regional exchange, but the majority of the exchange's trading volume is derived from transactions of NYSE-AMEX- and Nasdaq-listed stocks. Because of the Intermarket Trading System, it is as easy to buy AT&T from the Boston or Chicago exchange as it is from the New York exchange. Stock-price quotes from the regional specialists are as competitive as, and sometimes better than, the New York quotes.

The Chicago Stock Exchange (CHX; formerly Midwest Stock Exchange)

Founded in 1882, this exchange grew through the mergers in 1949 and 1959 of several separate exchanges, including the Chicago, St. Louis, Cleveland, Minneapolis-St. Paul and New Orleans exchanges. Located in the heart of Chicago's financial district, it is the most active regional exchange by a considerable margin. With only 19 exclusive listings, it is obvious that the bulk of trading is in NYSE- and AMEX-listed companies. For more information, call or write the Chicago Stock Exchange (440 S. LaSalle St., Chicago, IL 60605; 312-663-2222).

The Pacific Stock Exchange

The Pacific Stock Exchange was formed in 1956 by the merger of the Los Angeles and the San Francisco exchanges. Separate trading floors still are maintained in each city, and most of the options trading takes place in San Francisco, while the majority of stock activity is in Los Angeles. The Pacific Exchange offers over 130 exclusive listings. Interestingly, the Pacific Exchange executes more trades than any other exchange that participates in the Intermarket Trading System except for the NYSE. However, the trades are for smaller volume amounts, so the Chicago Exchange enjoys a larger market share. The Pacific Exchange does have one big advantage: It is open 50 minutes later than all the other exchanges. For more information, call or write the Pacific Stock Exchange (301 Pine St., San Francisco, CA 94104; 415-393-4000 or 800-TALK-PSE).

The Philadelphia Stock Exchange

Founded in 1790 (two years before the NYSE), the Philadelphia Stock Exchange is the oldest organized stock exchange in the United States. During the years, it has merged with the Baltimore and Washington, D.C., exchanges. The Philadelphia Exchange has been very successful with options. Perhaps the best known is its foreign-currency option. The options are offered on the Japanese yen, Canadian dollar, Australian dollar, Swiss franc, French franc, Deutsche mark and British pound. Since 1971, when the U.S. dollar's value was no longer backed by gold, the options have provided valuable hedging tools in the volatile currency markets. For more information, call or write the Philadelphia Stock Exchange (1900 Market St., Philadelphia, PA 19103; 215-496-5000 or 800-THE-PHLX).

The Boston Stock Exchange

Founded in 1834, the Boston Stock Exchange is the third oldest stock exchange in the United States. While it has 127 exclusive listings, the majority of its trading volume is in NYSE issues. Located so close to New York, it always has had an identity problem; and considering the electronic linking of all the markets, it may have outlived its usefulness for purchasing stocks. However, because Boston is a major location for mutual-fund and money-management firms, the exchange may survive. For more information, call or write the Boston Stock Exchange (One Boston Place, 38th Floor, Boston, MA 02108; 617-723-9500).

The Cincinnati Stock Exchange

The Cincinnati Exchange has been around since 1885. While the exchange has no exclusive listings, it does offer a unique method of trading. In May 1978 Cincinnati began using the National Securities Trading System, which employs a computer to receive, store and display all orders entered into it. The system matches orders to see which can be executed and then completes them. Unlike a specialist, the computerized system makes no market judgments or pricing decisions and executes the orders on a first-come, first-served basis. The system is highly efficient and allows everyone to observe the size and the extent of the orders currently entered. Unfortunately, with recent computer innovations, the technological advantages of this system have become somewhat obsolete. For more information, call or write the Cincinnati Stock Exchange (36 E. 4th St., Suite 906, Cincinnati, OH 45202; 513-621-1410).

THE NASDAQ MARKET (FORMERLY THE OVER-THE-COUNTER MARKET)

Until recently, this market was known as the Over-the-Counter Market (OTC). The original market name, Over the Counter, dates back to the late 1700s when Wall Street was enjoying its first bull market and merchants, encouraged by increased activity, kept a small inventory of securities on hand that they sold over the counter along with their other goods. Unlike the NYSE and AMEX, which have physical exchange floors, the Nasdaq consists of thousands of securities houses located in hundreds of cities across the country. The securities transactions are handled by a communications network that links the securities houses with each other.

The Nasdaq market lists the largest number of securities—approximately 50,000. The types of securities traded on the Nasdaq market are bank stocks, insurance company stocks, U.S. government securities, municipal bonds, open-end investment company shares (mutual funds), railroad equipment trust certificates, most corporate bonds and tens of thousands of smaller companies' stocks. The market is comprised of securities that, for the most part, do not meet the more demanding listing requirements of the NYSE and the AMEX.

Virtually all brokerage firms that sell Nasdaq stocks belong to the National Association of Securities Dealers (NASD), which is a non-profit organization formed in cooperation with Congress and the Securities and Exchange Commission (SEC) to comply with the 1938 Maloney Act. The basic purpose of the NASD is to promote the investment banking and securities business, standardize industry trading practices, maintain high moral and ethical standards in securities trading, provide a representative body to consult with the government and investors on matters of importance, establish and enforce fair and equitable rules of securities trading and set up a disciplinary body capable of enforcing these provisions. The NASD also requires that member brokerage firms maintain quick assets (readily convertible assets on hand) in excess of current liabilities at all times.

The Nasdaq market as we know it today began February 5, 1971, with the formation of the National Association of Securities Dealers

Automated Quotations (Nasdaq) system, which is owned and operated by the NASD. The Nasdaq is a computerized system that provides brokers and dealers with price quotations for securities traded in the market. In less than three decades it has become the second largest market, and many times has bettered the NYSE in the total daily share volume.

Any stock wanting to be listed on the Nasdaq system must have the following:

- Total assets of at least $4 million, and capital and surplus of at least $2 million
- A bid price of $3 per share
- A public float of 100,000 shares with a market value of over $1 million
- At least 300 shareholders of record and two market makers
- Must pay a listing fee

On the NYSE and AMEX, the specialists create orderly markets in particular stocks; on the Nasdaq market *market makers* perform the same function. Through their computer terminals, market makers enter the highest prices at which they are willing to buy securities and the lowest prices at which they are willing to sell them. This is why Nasdaq stocks show two prices—the bid and the asked.

The *asked price* is the lowest price at which the market maker will sell a stock (i.e., the price the investor pays to buy the stock). The *bid* is the highest price at which the market maker will buy a stock (i.e., the price the investor will receive if he or she sells the stock). The *spread* is the difference between the bid and the asked price.

Understanding a Nasdaq Stock Transaction

If an investor wants to buy 100 shares of Fonar, she just calls her broker, who takes the order and sends it to the trading room. If the brokerage firm is a market maker in Fonar, it can execute the order as a principal. If the current bid on Fonar is $2.50 and the asked price is $2.56, the brokerage firm will sell the stock to the investor for $2.56 or perhaps $2.63 but will require no commission. If the brokerage firm is not a market maker, it will buy Fonar from a brokerage firm that is a market maker for the $2.50 price and sell it to the investor at $2.56 plus a commission of up to 10 percent of the stock cost.

Competition among the various Fonar market makers should guarantee investors the best price available.

The Nasdaq National Market System

In 1982 Nasdaq devised a new market called the National Market System, which has become the largest traded and most prominent Nasdaq market. It lists just under 3,000 stocks and is published daily in every major newspaper. To be listed in the Nasdaq National Market System, a company must have

- net tangible assets of $12 million or a net income of at least $400,000 and pretax income of $750,000 during the past fiscal year or two out of the past three years;
- a float of at least 500,000 shares;
- a market value for the float of at least $3 million;
- a minimum bid price of $5 (sometimes waived); and
- paid a listing fee.

OTC Pink Sheets

If a company doesn't meet even the minimum Nasdaq requirements, it becomes listed on the OTC pink sheets, a daily publication from the National Quotation Bureau that prints the bid and asked prices and the market makers.

When investing in stocks, make sure that you invest only in stocks that are listed on the NYSE, AMEX or Nasdaq because you can easily obtain accurate stock prices. In addition, these companies file quarterly and annual reports with the SEC. In Chapter 5 I will discuss the importance of these reports.

In 1989 the NASD introduced its OTC Bulletin Board, which is an electronic system listing the current bid and asked price of certain pink-sheet stocks. The jury still is out on whether this system will be a success. I recommend avoiding all pink-sheet stocks because it is difficult to accurately follow their stock prices. In many cases the spread between the bid and the asked price is outrageous.

Because these stocks are not required to file any quarterly or annual reports with the SEC, it is virtually impossible to obtain adequate information to make an educated decision on the quality of the stock. While not all pink-sheet stocks are bad investments and a

Figure 3.1 Dow Jones Industrials

Aluminum Corporation of America	Eastman Kodak Co.	Philip Morris
Allied-Signal, Inc.	Exxon Corporation	Procter & Gamble Co.
American Express Company	General Electric Company	Sears, Roebuck & Co.
AT&T	General Motors Corporation	Texaco, Inc.
Bethlehem Steel Corp.	Goodyear Tire & Rubber Co.	Union Carbide Corp.
Boeing Company	IBM	United Technologies Corp.
Caterpillar Inc.	International Paper Co.	Walt Disney Co.
Chevron Corporation	McDonald's Corporation	Westinghouse Electric Corp.
Coca-Cola Enterprises, Inc.	Merck & Co., Inc.	F. W. Woolworth Company
DuPont	Minnesota Mining & Mfg. Co.	
	J. P. Morgan & Co.	

few even become listed on Nasdaq, pink-sheet stocks have been involved in the vast majority of penny-stock scams and violations.

Often a pink-sheet company will claim that it will shortly be listed on Nasdaq. Occasionally, they do become listed. Many times, however, this is just talk.

STOCK INDEXES AND THEIR MARKET EFFECT

A stock index (or average) measures and reports value changes in representative stock groupings. As an investor, you can compare the movement of your stock to a particular index to see if your investment is performing better or worse than the average. For example, if you own a stock on the NYSE, you may want to compare it to the Dow Jones Industrials, which is probably the premier index.

The Dow Jones Industrial Average (DJIA) is considered the barometer of the stock market. The Dow Jones average was created by Charles H. Dow, the first editor of *The Wall Street Journal*, on July 3, 1884; it consisted of 11 stocks—9 railroad companies and 2 industrial companies.

On March 26, 1896, Dow created his first Dow Jones Industrial Average, which was made up of 12 industrial stocks. In 1928, the average was changed to 30 stocks, and even though the companies composing the average have been changed many times, the number has remained at 30. The 30 current Dow Jones Industrial stocks are shown in Figure 3.1.

Figure 3.2   Dow Jones Industrial Average: 1993

One of the things that has scared the small investor since the 1987 crash has been the tremendous volatility of the Dow Jones Industrials since then. Figure 3.2 delineates the changes in the Dow Jones Industrials for 1993. Because it is followed by so many analysts, if this index indicates either an upward or downward movement, it can influence investors into continuing the trend—which becomes a self-fulfilling prophecy. If everyone believes the market is in trouble and fails to invest, then the market will be in trouble. I believe that many investors spend too much time worrying about the volatility of the

Dow Jones Industrials over the short term. They should be more interested in long-term trends.

You may also want to follow the transportation or the utilities averages if you own stocks in these industries. The Dow Jones Transportation Average (DJTA) is an index composed of 20 stocks in the transportation industry, including railway, airline and trucking companies. The Dow Jones Utility Average (DJUA) includes 15 stocks in the public utility industry, such as gas and electric companies.

The New York and American exchanges and the Nasdaq market each have a composite index. The composite indexes express in dollars and cents the change in each market as a whole. The NYSE composite index covers the price movements of all common stocks listed on that exchange. Point changes in the index are converted to dollars and cents to provide a meaningful measure of changes in the average price of listed stocks.

I like to follow three indexes that you can find daily in *The Wall Street Journal* and in most major newspapers. The NYSE Advance and Decline Ratio shows the number of stocks up and down on a particular day. The New Highs and Lows is printed both daily and weekly. It lists stocks from all three exchanges, and I follow the new lows closely to locate potential turnaround companies. The Price Percentage Movers indicates both the top percent winners and losers. By following this index, you can discover some of the more volatile cyclical stocks.

The stock indexes should be used as a quick overall guide, but investors shouldn't waste too much time worrying about the daily volatility of the market. Instead, their emphasis should be placed on determining longer-term trends. The investors' time can be spent more profitably by researching companies to ascertain which stocks have better investment potential because of the company's quality.

CHAPTER

4

Understanding the Investment Process

Buying a stock and watching your money grow is a thrilling experience, and it is the basic reason for investing. This enticing concept sometimes works and sometimes doesn't. How did the idea of investing in a company begin in the first place? It started because someone needed money for his or her company and didn't have any other way to raise it. Let's look at the reasons why a company decides to offer part of its ownership to the public.

WHY A COMPANY DECIDES TO SELL STOCK

While most companies are started with capital from the founder or his or her family or friends, almost always there comes a time when more capital is needed. Perhaps it is necessary to research a new idea for a product or develop the product so it can be marketed. The company may want to expand its marketing areas or consolidate or modernize various production and corporate offices into a larger, more efficient facility. Whatever the reason, the company must obtain additional capital to execute the change. Many times banks are hesitant to lend money to a company when it needs capital (a Catch-22 situation), so the company's only alternative may be to sell shares of stock to the public. Buying stock gives the investor the opportunity to purchase part of the ownership of the company and grants the investor the right to some voice in how the company is run.

Before the company makes the decision to offer stock, it must consider the advantages and disadvantages of going public. The advantages include the following:

- The main advantage is obtaining needed capital.
- The capital can be used in many beneficial ways, including increasing working capital, expanding research and development, extending the company's marketplace, hiring additional employees, updating or expanding facilities, retiring existing debt, providing capital for acquisitions or increasing the company's net worth.
- The shares can be used to attract key management or technical people or motivate the current work force through stock-option or profit-sharing programs.
- Through the public offering, the company gains prestige with more than 100,000 brokers nationwide, increases its visibility through public relations press releases sent to national media and enhances its relationship with its bankers.
- A public offering also assigns a value to the company in case it is entertaining the idea of merging or being acquired. It designates a price for the private shares held by the original owners and management.
- Public shares can be used as collateral and borrowed against or sold when additional monies are needed in the future.
- A public offering will expand the company's borrowing capability and allow it to obtain favorable credit terms for future borrowing.
- For the founders of the company, a public offering provides the fulfillment, usually after many years of hard work, of wealth, power and prestige.

The disadvantages of going public include the following:

- Going public involves a relatively high expenditure of capital (from $25,000 to $300,000, depending on the size of the offering) with no certain guarantee that enough investors will want to buy the stock to make it valuable.
- The company will lose privacy. It must make public information about its sales, profits, losses, mode of operation, competitive position, managements' salaries, lawsuits and many other aspects affecting the company.

- Additional costs will be involved to keep the shareholders up to date with annual reports, quarterly reports, press releases, etc. After going public, most companies are required to file quarterly and annual reports (10-Q and 10-K) with the SEC. Legal costs usually skyrocket because of the need for additional legal expertise to write the regulatory reports. Typical expenses for reports and legal fees can cost as much as $100,000 or more a year.
- The company's management loses some of its decision-making control to the shareholders for major decisions such as conducting a merger or changing its name.
- More pressure is exerted on the company to show increased sales and earnings each year.

Going public is an important decision for a company to make. In many cases, if the company wants to continue to grow, going public may be the only logical choice. This works to the advantage of investors, for it gives them the opportunity to invest in some great companies.

SPECIALIZING IN ONE AREA RATHER THAN IN MANY

One of the biggest mistakes an investor can make is spending too much time looking at too many different types of investments. The investor ends up spreading himself or herself too thin and learns a little about a lot and not a lot about anything. The average investor has only so much time to devote to developing an understanding of investments. To be a more efficient investor, I believe that you can spend your time better by specializing in a particular type of investment that interests you.

☐   **RULE 3**   ☐

Don't be a jack-of-all-trades and a master of none—specialize in one specific area.

Once you start to learn about a certain type of investment, you begin to realize just how much you don't know; this can be overwhelming. There is much to assimilate, such as how the investment works, why it goes up and down in value, how to research that investment, what criteria point to a more potentially successful investment and what is the best way to make money in that investment. It takes a long time to master just one area of investments. I learned that years ago and devoted my time to stocks under $10 per share. I believe that specializing in an area I understand has been a major contribution to the success of *The CHEAP Investor* newsletter.

You can choose many different ways to specialize. For example, you can restrict your investigations to a certain type of investment, such as common stocks, options, futures or mutual funds. This book is limited to common stocks with a small section on warrants. However, approximately 60,000 common stocks are listed on the NYSE, AMEX, Nasdaq, pink sheets and foreign exchanges. I decided to focus on stocks under $10 listed on the NYSE, AMEX and Nasdaq, which reduced the number to under 5,000 stocks. Then I specialized further by looking only at quality stocks (those of profitable, established companies), which then narrowed the base to less than 2,000 stocks, a more manageable number.

If you think that is still too many stocks, you may want to restrict your research to certain industries, specific prices or particular exchanges. This will reduce the number of companies to an amount that you can comfortably investigate. Spending your time researching various companies in the area in which you specialize can be extremely profitable. Focusing your attention on a much smaller area may allow you to surprise your friends and yourself with the competent opinions you are able to voice on those stocks. (Your opinion, if well researched, may be more knowledgeable than that of many "experts.")

THE GREED/FEAR TRAP

During the bull market of the early 1990s, we witnessed some tremendous increases in stock prices. Many investors saw their stocks move up quickly and continued to watch as the prices fell back to or below their original purchase prices. Those investors showed fantastic paper profits, but they didn't take them. When the stock prices started to fall, the investors figured the prices would rise again. Instead, the investors' paper profits disappeared, and they lost their opportunities to make nice profits.

Figure 4.1   The Greed/Fear Trap

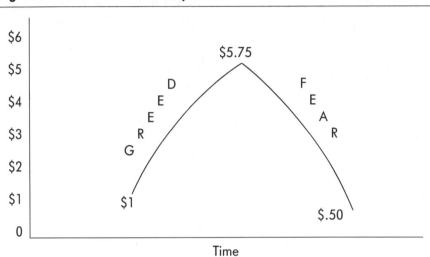

Don't fall victim to the greed/fear trap.

What happened? I call it the greed/fear trap. Figure 4.1 illustrates this problem. The investor buys a quality, low-priced stock at $1 per share. The stock price starts to rise, hitting $2, $3, $4, $5, up to a high of $5.75. The investor now has a tremendous profit and decides to sell when the stock hits $6.

The investor has held the stock because of greed. With every upward movement in the stock price, the investor congratulates himself or herself and figures out how much money he or she has made. Perhaps the stock moved up fast and the investor thinks, "Gee, if it has moved up this much in only two months, imagine how high it will be after four months!"

This kind of greed in itself is not wrong. After all, why would anyone want to invest in a stock except for the greedy reason of making money? However, if greed keeps the investor from realizing a profit, it becomes a liability. The final mistake the investor makes is letting this greed cause him or her to enter a sell order at $6. The investor wants to make a few more cents profit per share. It doesn't matter that the stock has already made a fantastic profit, moving from

Figure 4.2 Stop Loss Prices

Stock Price	$2.00	$3.00	$4.00	$5.00	$6.00	$7.00	$8.00	$9.00	$10.00
Stop Loss	1.63	2.13	3.13	4.13	4.88	5.88	6.88	7.88	8.88

$1 to $5.75 or +475 percent. If Murphy's Law (namely, anything that can go wrong will go wrong) is operating, the stock will never reach $6 before falling.

Greed has kept the investor from taking a profit because he or she is sure that the stock will continue to rise. Normally, when a stock moves up fast, it falls even faster. Once the stock starts to fall, the investor rationalizes, "I can't sell it at $5 because it was at $5.75 only yesterday; and I'm sure it will go back up." Then as the stock continues to fall, the investor becomes afraid to take the profit and reasons, "I can't sell the stock for only $3 when it was $5.75. It will go up again, and I'll miss out if I sell now." This continues until the stock usually ends up below the original purchase price—perhaps at $.50. Then the unhappy investor just wishes the stock would go back up to the original $1 purchase price so he or she can break even. (I'm sure that anyone who has ever invested can at one time or another recognize himself or herself as a victim of the greed/fear trap.)

PROTECTING YOURSELF FROM THE GREED/FEAR TRAP

Smart investors recognize how easy it is to fall into the greed/fear trap and learn to avoid it. They can protect themselves with a *stop loss order,* which is an order placed with their broker to sell the stock if the price drops to a specified point. As the stock price moves up, they raise the stop loss; but if the price experiences a serious drop, the stock will automatically be sold, and they will realize a profit.

For example, if you bought a stock at $1 and it moved up to $2, you could call your broker and enter a stop loss order for $1.63. The stop loss should automatically sell your stock if it drops to $1.63. You have made a nice profit and have protected yourself in case the stock price drops further. As the stock price continues to move upward, your stop loss should be adjusted. Figure 4.2 shows suggested stop loss prices.

Notice that the suggested stop loss for $2 is $1.63. Why not $1.75? Because that is where most investors would put it. To avoid a problem with selling your stock because too many other orders have also been entered, refrain from setting stop losses on the even dollar, $.50 or $.25 amounts. At the $2, $3 and $4 prices the stop loss is $.87 below the price; however, at the $6 through $10 level, it is $1.12 less. Why? Because the higher the stock price moves, the more volatility the stock has.

You want to protect your profit, yet you also don't want the stock sold just because the price jumped around a little. At higher prices, the major resistance point is usually at the dollar level. Therefore, if your stock hits $9, it may back off to $8 before continuing upward. If your stop loss had been set at $8.13, the stock would have been sold; and while you would have made a nice profit, there was potential for more. As you can see, it is a delicate job to set the stop loss high enough to keep your profit, but not so high that the stock gets sold when the price backs off somewhat.

If your stock moves up nicely and you enjoy a 50 percent profit in a few months, you are never "wrong" to take a profit on a stock. Granted, the stock may continue upward and you could have made even more profit; however, too many of us get caught up by greed, holding on for just a little more and ending up right back where we started (or even worse). Don't let yourself get caught; protect your profits. Take them when you think it is wise, and don't look back and berate yourself because you could have made more. That just wastes time and energy. You'll be busy enough analyzing potential investments and checking on the ones you have already made.

CHAPTER

5

Analyzing Stocks Easily
and Profitably

An investor's ultimate goal is to discern which investment affords the greatest profit potential. Some people let their brokers decide for them. Others pick a name that sounds familiar and has the ring of quality. A few have even tried the dart board method of choosing stocks. (The investor throws a dart at a listing of stocks and buys the one that is hit.)

Choosing an investment is easy. However, if the investor wants to actually determine if the stock is a good investment, then he or she must analyze it. Making the effort to carefully check out an investment before buying it positions an individual in a select category of investors—the smart ones.

FUNDAMENTAL AND TECHNICAL ANALYSIS

While many variations exist, there are two major ways to analyze stocks. *Fundamental analysis* covers the study of all relevant financial information about a company that can influence the future course of its stock price. *Technical analysis* examines all factors related to the actual supply and demand for the company's stock.

Fundamental Analysis

This type of stock analysis evaluates the worthiness of a security by examining the company's tangible assets and financial strength. It focuses on elements such as book value, earnings per share and price-earnings (PE) ratio, along with the stock's price in relation to its 52-week high-low range. Fundamental analysis considers past records of assets, earnings, sales, products, management and markets when predicting future trends in the company's success or failure. Fundamental analysts may consider outside factors that could influence the company, such as the economic situation, government policy and the company's stature within its industry. The primary source of the data used in the analysis is the company's own financial statements, which can be found in its annual, 10-K, 10-Q and quarterly reports.

Fundamental analysis received much publicity, which created a great following during the 1930s depression when stocks were selling at perhaps 10 to 20 percent of their real value. *Security Analysis and Techniques* by Benjamin Graham and David Dodd, first printed in 1934, is the bible of fundamental analysis. In the book's preface the authors wrote of their decision to place "much emphasis upon distinguishing the investment from the speculative approach, upon setting up sound and workable tests of safety and upon an understanding of the rights and true interests of investors in senior securities and owners of common stock." Investors wanted to read that during the 1930s, and I believe the same holds true today.

The premise of fundamental analysis is to examine a company's financial statement and other relevant information to discover if it is selling significantly below its worth. If so, the investor purchases the stock and waits until the rest of the world recognizes the stock's value. Sooner or later the stock price should move up closer to its true value. When the stock price goes up because everyone wants to buy it, that is the time to sell and use fundamental analysis to locate another undervalued company.

T. Boone Pickens uses fundamental analysis to locate potential takeover candidates. Evaluating the fundamentals of a company allows Pickens to determine if the breakup value is greater than the stock price. (The *breakup value* is what the stock could be worth if all the assets of the company were sold.) Pickens has used this type of analysis very successfully to identify profitable takeover candidates.

Figure 5.1 Price Chart

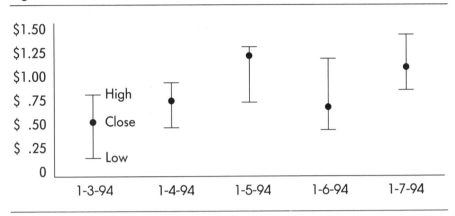

Technical Analysis

Technical analysis usually thrives during times of economic prosperity or during bullish periods when stock prices are rising and trading profits are easy to make. In such times many analysts may revise their view of fundamental analysis and consider it out-of-date.

Technical analysts (or technicians) study all the factors related to the supply and demand of stocks. Through the use of stock charts, technicians seek various indicators that herald the change in the price or volume of a particular stock. The major advantage of using technical analysis is that it shows a picture of the stock's price history. The simplest type of chart is a bar chart that indicates the high price, low price and closing price for the time period that can be calculated on a daily, weekly, monthly or yearly basis. Figure 5.1 is a bar chart that shows a week's worth of high, low and closing prices. A volume chart for a week may look like the one in Figure 5.2.

In technical analysis the investor is looking for patterns that could indicate which way the stock price will move. Figure 5.3 shows four basic patterns used in this type of analysis.

Technicians believe that because people make markets and people don't change that much, under similar conditions they will repeat their previous actions. Therefore, technical analysis involves the study of statistics for certain transactions to determine the direction of the future price of a stock or market. The technicians have concluded that those stocks or markets contain enough predictable elements to ensure the profitability of such studies over a period of time.

Figure 5.2   Volume Chart

While a technician's charts are easy to read, using them correctly is more difficult. The analyst must anticipate where the stock is going, and the chart can be misleading, especially if it just shows a short period of time. Charting a stock for a period of months or years may show cyclical trends that occur around the same time each year. For example, a stock's price may rise shortly before it announces its quarterly dividend and then may fall rapidly thereafter. Determining such a pattern can give the investor an added profit-making edge.

Technicians study the market using various indicators, including the evaluation of the economic variables within a market. Many stocks move with the market because they react to various demand-and-supply forces. That is, if investors want to buy more stock than is available, the price will go up. If more stock is being sold than there are buyers for the stock, the price will go down. Technical analysis can work well with stocks that tend to follow the market in general, such as the Dow Jones index stocks and other blue chips. However, I have found that this type of analysis doesn't work well with lower-priced stocks because bargain stocks don't consistently follow the market.

Some technicians follow the trading volume, for they believe that it can indicate whether or not a stock or a market is healthy. Presumably, the stock or market price will follow the volume trend. However, I have found that this is not always true.

An interesting variation of technical analysis is the *odd-lot theory,* which is based on contrary opinion. The theory concludes that historically, the odd-lot traders (small investors who trade in less than 100-share quantities) are usually guilty of bad timing. When odd-lot volume rises

Figure 5.3   Basic Four Patterns Used in Technical Analysis

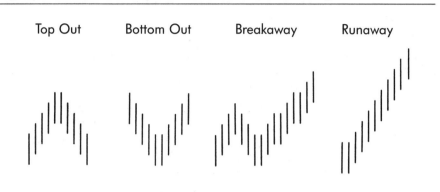

Top Out   Bottom Out   Breakaway   Runaway

in an up stock market, the odd-lot analyst views it as a sign of technical weakness that signals a market reversal. Basically, the technician determines what the odd-lot traders are doing and does the opposite.

You may have heard of a fourth theory for investment called *Random Walk.* This investment philosophy discounts both fundamental and technical analysis. It concludes that at least in the short run, the market pricing is completely at random; there is no pattern because every price movement is independent of the previous one. So much for technical analysis! It also assumes that the market is efficient, so there are no underpriced or overpriced stocks. That dismisses fundamental analysis. So what is left? Well, you can always use the dartboard to pick your stocks. However, my best success has come from using fundamental analysis.

Comparing Fundamental and Technical Analysis

Let's look at fundamental and technical analysis in action. In mid-1992 I recommended Global Marine, a NYSE stock selling at $1.13. Why? Because Global had strong fundamentals. Its year-end sales rose from $281 million to $315 million, and net income jumped from a loss of $36 million to a net income of $1 million. In addition, the company had reduced its long-term debt while its cash and assets had increased. The company was in the oil industry, and oil prices were at the low point of their cycle.

Despite the turnaround in its income statement, I believed the stock's price was exceedingly low. In fact, it was selling at its 52-week low. A technician looking at Global would not have been impressed with it because of its price's downward trend and low volume.

About a year later, Global Marine's price had moved from $1.13 to $5.25, and the trading volume started to shoot up. With the upswing in volume and price, many technicians began buying Global at a price almost five times what my subscribers paid for it! The stock hit a high of $5.75 before beginning its downward descent.

Global Marine is a prime example of the benefits of using fundamental analysis to discover a quality investment. Instead of waiting until a stock's price and volume increase dramatically on technical charts to indicate that it is a good buy, fundamental analysis allows the investor to buy the stock at a much lower price. That is the main reason I use fundamental analysis and perhaps why *The CHEAP Investor* has recommended so many stocks well before the Wall Street analysts become interested in them.

LEARNING FROM ANNUAL, 10-K, 10-Q AND QUARTERLY REPORTS AND PRESS RELEASES

To analyze a stock, you need several publications that you can obtain directly from the company by either calling or writing to request its annual report, the 10-K and 10-Q reports, its latest quarterly report and any press releases. The information in these reports can help you determine whether or not a stock is a potentially profitable investment.

Annual Reports

The formal yearly report of a corporation's financial condition that the SEC requires to be distributed to shareholders is the annual report. In addition to financial reports and notes from an independent certified public accountant, the report commonly contains a summary of the products or services, a progress report, comments from the president and chairperson on the company's financial and industry status and reports on corporate expansion and new products.

Most annual reports are designed by the company's advertising or public relations department to promote the company to the reader. Generally written in easy-to-understand language, the annual report explains the company's products and goals. It can be very basic and printed in black and white, or it can be very flashy and include multiple colors on glossy paper with attractive pictures to impress shareholders. A company with poor financial results may invest in an extremely expensive-looking annual report, hoping that it will give the impression that it is a good investment. Don't be fooled.

Financial Statements   While annual reports vary greatly, they all contain financial statements that are audited, written records of the company's financial status. The financial statement consists of five parts: (1) the consolidated balance sheet, (2) the income statement, (3) the statement of changes in financial position, (4) the statement of retained earnings and (5) notes to the financial statements.

Consolidated Balance Sheet   A company's balance sheet presents its financial position in detail. It shows the balance of its various types of assets, liabilities and shareholder equity as of a specific date (usually the end of the month). The *assets* are basically what the company owns, the *liabilities* are what it owes and the *shareholder's equity* is the value of the stock after all the liabilities are subtracted from the assets.

Income Statement   This report provides information concerning the total revenues, costs, expenses and net earnings from operations.

Statement of Changes in Financial Position   An audited report, this statement presents information concerning the company's operating, financing and investing activities. The statement indicates any changes in the company's financial position during the year.

Statement of Retained Earnings   This is a combined statement of the company's yearly income and retained earnings. *Retained earnings* is the total amount of cumulative net profits reinvested in the corporation after the payment of dividends.

Notes to the Financial Statements   This final report provides an explanation of specific items in the financial statement. The notes are extremely important, for they may contain positive or negative information that could have a significant impact on the company. As a potential investor, you will want to read them carefully.

What To Look For in the Annual Report   There is no standardized form for annual reports, so I can only generalize. On the inside of the annual report's front cover there usually is a corporate profile detailing the company's main areas of business. If the company's earnings are very positive, the report will probably contain a section on selected financial data comparing three to five years of sales (or revenues), net income, net income per share and the number of shares outstanding. Have the sales and net income improved compared to the previous year or years?

Financial Highlights Section   Many annual reports contain a financial highlights section that details sales, earnings, assets, liabilities and shareholder's equity. Look for increases in the assets and in the shareholder's equity and decreases in the liabilities. Read the notes below the financial data to see if there is anything extremely positive or negative.

Letter to the Shareholders   The letter to the shareholders is written by the chairperson of the board and/or the president. It details what has happened to the company during the past year and presents the goals that the company hopes to accomplish during the next year. Typically, the letter is extremely positive, looking on the bright side regardless of the company's performance during the past year.

Notes to the Financial Statement   If you like what you have seen so far, find the section in the financial statement called the "Notes to the Financial Statement" and read it carefully. Near the end of the annual report should be a section on litigation. It is not unusual for lawsuits to be brought against a company; however, you should investigate to see whether the company has insurance to cover the cost if it loses any lawsuit. If the company is suing another company or individual for a large amount of money, this could prove extremely positive if the company wins. (In fact, MCI received a big boost by suing AT&T and winning.)

Accountant's Letter   Look at the accountant's letter. Reading this letter will often give you some insight, especially the paragraph starting with "In our opinion." Is the company's accountant a major company? If so, that is positive.

Number of Shareholders   The number of shareholders can also be important, and a stock with at least 1,000 shareholders is best. A large number of shareholders indicates that there are many small shareholders. When selling occurs in a stock with only a small number of shareholders, it can cause the stock to be more volatile, especially on the downside.

Market Information   The market-information section indicates which exchange the stock is traded on and its symbol and gives two years (by quarters) of its high and low prices. The example below shows that the high and the low price may vary quite a bit depending on the quarter.

High and Low Bid Prices
(Year-end December 31, 1993)

	High	Low
Fourth quarter	$6.50	$3.13
Third quarter	3.50	2.75
Second quarter	5.38	2.25
First quarter	3.88	3.75

High and Low Bid Prices
(Year-end December 31, 1992)

	High	Low
Fourth quarter	$5.00	$2.75
Third quarter	4.25	3.50
Second quarter	5.00	2.13
First quarter	3.00	2.38

It is not uncommon for a stock to trade at higher prices during certain quarters. In the previous example a stock has traded for a higher price in the second and fourth quarters. If you check the company's sales and earnings for these quarters, you may find a correlation between the sales and earnings and the stock price. Many companies experience seasonal sales, and those quarters may be historically better than others.

Form 10-K

This report is filed with the SEC by all companies with at least 500 shareholders and $1 million or more in assets (basically all companies listed on NYSE, AMEX and Nasdaq). The SEC requires that certain information must be listed in the 10-K and that it must be filed within 90 days after the close of the fiscal year. Because the 10-K is written by the financial department and sent to the SEC, it gives more explicit information about the company and its divisions, finances and products than does the annual report.

The 10-K may seem complicated at first, but it becomes easier to read with practice. It includes the following information about the company:

- Industry
- Competitors
- Regulations
- Patents and trademarks
- Accessibility of raw materials
- Locations of each division, office, franchise, etc.
- Order backlog
- Research and development
- Environmental regulations
- Employees
- Foreign and domestic operations
- Export sales
- Description of properties, including location, size, cost and lease expiration date
- Marketing
- Employment agreements
- Full information on all legal proceedings
- Company stock-market information
- Complete annual financial statements
- Liquidity and capital resources
- Management's description and analysis of the financial condition and results of operations
- Inflation and price changes
- Expenses—e.g., why they changed and specific factors that caused the change
- Information and background on the directors and executive officers
- Executive compensation, including bonuses
- Profit-sharing, bonus and retirement plans
- Employee stock ownership, including the number of shares owned and the price paid by all officers and directors
- Information on various types of securities offered by the company

What is important to the investor? While all this information is interesting, some is more important to the stock price than others. If you don't have the annual report, then check the 10-K's financial statements; look for improvements. Read through the litigation to determine if there are any lawsuits that could either be very positive or negative for the company. Look at the stock market information to see if the price has any cyclical tendencies.

Check the management's compensation. Is it out of line with the company's finances? (Many companies have been bled dry by outlandish management salaries and stock-option or bonus programs.) The 10-K will contain the pertinent information if a Form 8-K has recently been filed with the SEC. A Form 8-K is required by the SEC following any event that affects the company's financial situation.

Learn if any warrants are outstanding. If so, what is the exercise price and the expiration date? Does the company plan a public or private offering of stock? In either case this could affect the price of the stock, for there will be more shares outstanding to dilute the value of the stock once the offering is completed or the warrant is exercised.

Always check the company's cash situation. If the cash assets are extremely low or the company is in a deficit position, the company may have to raise capital in the near future with a public or private offering that could severely weaken the current share's value.

Form 10-Q

This report is filed with the SEC 45 days after the end of the quarter. It is similar to the 10-K but much smaller. It, of course, presents the latest quarterly financial results. Check these numbers for positive or negative changes that should be taken into consideration when analyzing the company's investment potential.

The 10-Q contains the management's analysis of the quarter, any 8-K filings and the notes to the financial statements. All these should be examined. Basically, you are looking for any changes in the company's overall picture.

Quarterly Report

Usually one folded page, the quarterly report is sent to the shareholders to describe the current financial condition of the company. It contains the sales, net income, net income per share, number of shares outstanding and sometimes the shareholder's equity and compares it with the previous year's quarter. Analyze the figures for improvements. A short letter to the shareholders may be included. It may comment on the quarterly figures and describe any new developments during the past three months.

Press Releases

If the company also sent press releases or product information, you can read them to help you analyze the company.

GETTING THE FACTS BEFORE YOU INVEST

Many people lose money in the stock market because they invest based on the word of a relative, friend or broker. Often the information is completely wrong because each time it was passed from one person to another, something was added or deleted. If it was passed through enough people, the original information has probably been totally distorted. Even brokers experience problems, for many times they don't analyze a stock themselves but rely on their brokerage firm's analysts. This is fine except that the analysts may not have the time to update their information as often as they should, so the information the broker gets may be obsolete.

If you have an annual report, a 10-K, a 10-Q, a quarterly report and press releases, you probably have as much or more information than most stockbrokers and analysts have. Using that information wisely can make the difference between making and losing money. By doing your research first, you will know that the information is accurate and that you have increased your odds for a profit.

FINDING THE NEXT SUPERSTOCK

Taking the time to obtain the various company reports, reading them carefully and analyzing the stock's strong and weak points to see if it is a good buy can be well worth the effort. This is what I do, and it has proven to be a very successful method.

My ultimate goal when researching a company's stock is to find one with perfect criteria. The company must provide superior products or services. Its management team must possess the expertise to efficiently market that product or service, strive to improve sales and earnings, continue expansion with new products or services and search for new markets to penetrate. If the company's stock is at a good low price, it fulfills the qualifications for the next potential superstock.

The following are the three key items that can almost guarantee a stock-price jump:

1. The company is producing record sales.
2. The company is achieving record earnings.
3. The company's stock price is near its 52-week low.

Several of my big stock winners fit these criteria when I researched them. Here are a few of them:

Company Name	Recommended Price	High Since Recommendation
Envirodyne Industries	$2.81	$80.00 (buyout)
Grolier, Inc.	1.81	27.50 (buyout)
Arrow Electronics	3.75	43.00
Atari Corporation	1.00	12.75
Acclaim Entertainment	3.13	31.75

My statistics indicate that if you find a stock that satisfies the previously mentioned three criteria, your chances of the stock moving upward are more than 90 percent. If the company continues to achieve record sales and earnings, the chances are excellent that the stock price will soar. The great advantage of this approach is that you buy a stock way before the Wall Street analysts are interested. In fact, by the time they become interested in the stock (because it has moved up so high), it will be time for you to think about taking your profit. If you follow my lead and carefully analyze the fundamentals of any stock you are considering for an investment, perhaps you can find the next superstock and reap a tremendous profit as well.

CHAPTER

6

Mastering Stocks under $10

For more than 15 years I taught about investing in quality, low-priced stocks or as I say, CHEAP stocks. The small investor with a limited amount of capital obviously needs a higher percent of return than an investor with a large amount of investment capital. For example, if a small investor with only $3,000 and a large investor with $100,000 invest in a security with a guaranteed annual return of 10 percent, the small investor receives only $300 per year while the large investor collects $10,000.

Large investor: $100,000   10 percent = $10,000
Small investor: $3,000   10 percent = $300

Because the smaller investor is starting with a more modest amount of capital, he or she needs a higher rate of return (30, 40 or 50 percent) to help that capital grow. I have spent years researching differently priced stocks to find which ones may be more advantageous for the small investor. Through the practical application of various investment theories, I have concluded that CHEAP stocks offer a far greater growth potential, which the small investor needs. The higher-priced, blue chip stocks have, for the most part, already experienced their major growth cycle and thus do not provide a high enough rate of return. In fact, many of those stocks tend to be overpriced, and their prices probably will decrease.

☐   **RULE 5**   ☐

Don't lose money by investing in the wrong-priced stocks.

When investors buy higher-priced stocks, they encounter two obstacles to success. The first is that they can't afford to buy as many shares, and the commission fees can eliminate a good portion of their profit. The second obstacle is that many higher-priced stocks are so expensive that it is virtually impossible for the stocks to double in price. The CHEAP stocks offer a much greater growth potential than the long-established, high-priced stocks.

TREMENDOUS POTENTIAL VERSUS BLUE CHIPS

Again and again I have seen quality, low-priced stocks far outpace the blue chips, and I believe that it is much easier for a company such as Arrow Electronics (NYSE stock symbol ARW) to move from $3.75 to $7.50 than for IBM (NYSE stock symbol IBM) to double from $110 to $220. I have discovered that people who made fortunes owning today's blue chip stocks bought them years ago when the stocks were much cheaper and the investors could buy many more shares.

The small investor who has only $3,000 to invest must have his or her money work hard. While it may be tempting to buy blue chip stocks because they are "safer," they are so expensive that $3,000 will not buy many shares. Also, what may be a safe blue chip today can easily be a loser tomorrow. *Any* stock carries risk.

☐   **RULE 6**   ☐

To make profits, carefully consider the number of shares you control.

For example, you have $3,000 to invest. You can either buy Arrow at $3.75 or IBM at $110. As you can see, you would be able to purchase 800 shares of Arrow and not quite 28 shares of IBM.

$3,000 ÷ $3.75 per share for Arrow = 800 shares
$3,000 ÷ $110 per share for IBM = 28 shares

If both stocks rose $1, your profit would be much greater with Arrow than with IBM because you can buy more shares. As you can see, the more shares you own, the higher your profit.

800 shares of Arrow × $1 = $800
28 shares of IBM × $1 - $ 28

Although the Wall Street media report stock movements in points, I believe that when comparing blue chip stocks to stocks under $10, it is important to figure your profits in percentages rather than in points. Think about it; when it comes to financial matters, almost everyone uses percentages. The IRS taxes your income by a variable percent, your bank lends money to buy a new home or car and charges a certain percent interest and even your credit card company expects you to pay a percentage finance charge. Doesn't it make sense to look at your investment profits in percentages, too?

It's easy to be impressed by a stock that has jumped a few points in one day. Because blue chip stocks cost so much, the actual profit may not be as great as it seems. Wall Street gets excited when IBM moves up five points to $115, and the jump will be reported on almost all the business news programs. However, a $4 stock that jumps up $.50 is usually forgotten. In fact, IBM moved up less than 5 percent, while the $4 stock rose 13 percent! Which would you rather have owned?

☐ **RULE 7** ☐

Always look at profits and losses in percentages, not in points.

In the previous example, if Arrow increased by only $.75 and IBM jumped up $15, it might look like IBM had performed better. If you figure out the profit percentages, however, you will see a different story; Arrow's $.75 increase is a 36 percent profit, and IBM's huge $15 increase is a mere 14 percent profit.

800 Arrow shares × $.75 increase = $1,067 profit
$1,067 profit ÷ $3,000 purchase price = 36 percent
28 IBM shares × $15 increase = $420 profit
$420 profit by $3,000 purchase price = 14 percent

Of course, because you are comparing the same amount of investment ($3,000), it is pretty easy to see which stock gave you the greater profit. However, it would be rare that you would invest the same amount of money in all your stocks. Therefore, looking at the percent of profit is the only accurate way to compare just how well your investments have done.

These examples illustrate three important points:

1. *Many people lose money in the stock market because they invest in the wrong-price stocks.* Typically, you can make more money with a quality $3.75 stock than with a blue chip, $110 stock, and the growth potential is far greater with the growing $3.75 stock than with the mature $110 stock.
2. *An important key to making money in the stock market is the number of shares you control.* A $3,000 investment can control 800 shares of a $3.75 stock and less than 28 shares of a $110 stock.
3. *Always look at profits and losses in percentages, not points.* If you had just looked at how many points Arrow and IBM had risen, you would have been tempted to say that IBM had done quite a bit better than Arrow. In reality, Arrow Electronics was a more profitable investment.

LOCATING A CHEAP INVESTMENT

Finding the companies to research as potential investments involves actively searching for them. Look at the companies in the area where you live. It is extremely easy to get information and see how well a company's product is doing when it is located nearby. You can just call or stop into its business office to request information. I first became aware of Champion Parts (Nasdaq stock symbol CREB) because I passed the home office every day on my way to work. I recommended the stock in the first half of 1992 at $3.94 because it fit my investing criteria. In six months the stock almost doubled to $7.25.

Always be on the lookout for new companies when you are dining out, traveling or just socializing. If you are impressed by a company's new product or service, chances are good that many others will be impressed as well. The Boston Chicken franchise recently opened several restaurants in the Chicagoland area. I saw that they were extremely busy, and the food was excellent. When I asked the manager of one of the restaurants about the huge number of people buying chicken, he commented that it had been like that since the restaurant opened. He also mentioned that Boston Chicken was shortly going public for $20 per share. This turned out to be an extremely lucrative investment for those who bought the initial public offering, as the stock opened up for its first day of trading at $40 and quickly soared to a high of $56 before backing off to $37. Investors who bought the initial public offering at $20 were able to sell their stock as soon as the stock started to trade for at least a 100 percent profit!

A good source for potential investments is the business section in your local newspaper. You should also glance through *The Wall Street Journal, Investor's Business Daily* and *Barron's*. (All three newspapers should be available in your local library.)

Another way to find potential investments is to subscribe to a stock newsletter. Newsletters can be a great source of investments; however, you will want to do some research before you buy. Avoid newsletters that offer only one buy recommendation. If the newsletter has a good following, recommending only one stock will almost ensure that the stock will soar in price. However, the stock may move up so quickly that the average investor may not be able to buy at the low price. Make sure that the newsletter lists a specific buy price and gives the name, address and telephone number of the company so you can contact it

Figure 6.1   Potential Investments

52-Week		Company Name	Exchange	Price	Comment
High	Low				

for further information. If the newsletter gives only a broker's name and telephone number, be careful that he or she doesn't push you into buying something you really don't want.

Listing Stocks for Further Research

A good place to find and research bargain stocks is your main library. Using a copy of *The Wall Street Journal* or *Barron's*, search through the NYSE stocks, and make a list of all profitable companies under $10 near their 52-week low price. I use the format shown in Figure 6.1 to gather all the pertinent information. (When you hear of an interesting company, add it to this checklist.)

Once you have made the list of potential investments, then you can refer to other informational sources in the library such as *Standard & Poor's Stock Guide, Value Line, Standard & Poor's Stock Reports,* etc. These references will give you a synopsis of what a particular company does, its sales and earnings and its stock price over the past few years. Using that information, you can either cross the company off your potential investments list or add it to your investment-grade stocks list. (See Figure 6.2.)

The stocks on the investment-grade list need further research. Use all the techniques described in the previous chapter to analyze these stocks. Once you have carefully analyzed the investment candidates and eliminated those that don't qualify, you should have a group of quality, low-priced stocks from which to choose your investments.

Figure 6.2   Investment-Grade Stocks

52-Week		Company Name	Exchange	Price	Comment
High	Low				

Nasdaq Stocks

Buying and selling stocks that are listed on the Nasdaq market is different from buying and selling stocks listed on the New York and American exchanges. While stocks listed on the NYSE and AMEX are quoted with just one price, Nasdaq stocks have a bid and asked price. If a stock is listed as $1 bid and $1.13 asked, this means that if you wanted to buy the stock, you would pay the $1.13 asked price. If you wished to sell the stock, you would receive the $1 bid price. The $.13 difference between the bid and asked prices is called the *spread*.

The spread on a Nasdaq stock can indicate how actively the stock is traded. If a stock has a small spread, say $.03, then it trades a lot. However, if a stock doesn't trade very much, in many cases the spread will be large. It is not uncommon to see a thinly traded stock with a $.50 bid price and a $1 asked price. As an investor, don't even consider a stock with such a large spread. Because you would have to pay $1 to buy and would get only $.50 if you sold, the stock would have to move up $.50 or 100 percent before you break even!

Whenever you are considering a Nasdaq stock, always check the spread. Avoid all stocks with spreads greater than those listed in Figure 6.3.

OTC Pink-Sheet Stocks

Pink-sheet stocks are especially attractive investments to small investors. When a broker tells you about a great little company selling for only $.75 per share, many investors say, "Gee, the stock is so inexpensive. What the heck, what can I lose?" Unfortunately, you can lose your whole investment.

Figure 6.3   Target Nasdaq Stock Spreads

Stocks between $.125 and $.25	$ .03 spread
Stocks between $.26 and $.75	$ .03 to $.06 spread
Stocks between $.76 and $ 2.00	$.06 to $.125 spread
Stocks $2 and up	$.125 to $.25 spread

Many pink-sheet stocks may seem low priced but are actually tremendously overpriced! That $.75 stock may have a $.25 spread, which is outrageous. In addition, pink-sheet stocks do not list a 52-week high and low price, so it is very difficult to discover if the stock is near its high or low. Often a pink-sheet company has a stock value of $50 million (number of shares multiplied by stock price), yet it does not have the $4 million in assets to become listed on the Nasdaq. To me, that indicates that the stock is vastly overpriced.

A few years ago the Electronic Bulletin Board was created for certain pink-sheet stocks that generally are higher-quality stocks. This system allows brokers who subscribe to it access to the prices of these "elite" pink-sheet stocks. I do not recommend buying companies listed on the Electronic Bulletin Board because the price spreads are very wide, the stocks don't trade much and it's difficult to get accurate information on the companies.

When a broker calls you about any stock, always ask the following two questions:

1. *Where is the stock traded?* If the stock is traded on the NYSE, AMEX or Nasdaq, that's great. If it is a pink-sheet stock (or trades on the Vancouver exchange or the OTC Bulletin Board), say, "Thanks, but no thanks."
2. *Where is the stock's current price in relation to its 52-week high and low price?* Most investors fail to find out the answer to this question and wind up purchasing a stock at its high price. This can lead to disillusionment and selling at a much lower price.

A pink-sheet stock gets its name from the color of the pages of the National Quotation Bureau's publication that gives its bid and asked prices. Thousands of stocks do not meet the more stringent requirements to get listed on Nasdaq and are therefore listed on the pink sheets. Investors have five major problems with pink-sheet stocks.

1. *The vast majority of penny-stock scams are pink-sheet stocks.* Not all pink-sheet stocks are bad; however, they are the lowest rank of stocks. In general, if a stock doesn't have the assets to get listed on any of the more prestigious exchanges, it falls into the pink-sheet category. A pink-sheet stock may have a great story about its potential; however, I personally can't think of one pink-sheet company that has become a major corporation.

2. *It can be difficult to get any written information (including financial data) about a company.* A pink-sheet company does not have to give shareholders financial information, for it doesn't report to the SEC.

3. *You can't easily check a company's price yourself.* You won't find the company listed in any newspaper. You can't call most brokers to access the price on his or her computer. Normally, the only way you can find out the price is to call a broker who has received the printed pink sheets (which are yesterday's or last week's prices). In most cases you must rely on the broker who sold you the stock for the price quote. Because the broker knows that you have virtually no other way to check the price quote, the broker may be tempted to quote what he or she thinks you want to hear rather than what the actual price is.

4. *Because pink-sheet stocks are not widely traded, there may be a big spread between the price you pay to buy the stock and the price at which you can sell it.* In many cases you pay 50 percent more to buy, which means that your stock has to increase by 50 percent before you break even.

5. *Not only do pink-sheet stocks have wide spreads; generally only one brokerage firm controls the market for that stock.* If that brokerage firm goes under (which is not that uncommon), the stock may not even have a market, and the investor may end up with nothing except a worthless stock certificate. One such brokerage firm was the very successful Investor's Center, which had 27 offices across the United States and employed almost 1,000 brokers. A few years ago the Investor's Center closed its doors and left thousands of investors holding millions of dollars of stocks that were traded only by the Investor's Center. In 1990 the NASD and SEC entered into a

major campaign to severely restrict brokerage firms that specialize in penny stocks. This was the final straw for many firms. Blinder Robinson filed for Chapter 11, and Stuart James closed down, leaving their customers without a market to sell their millions of dollars' worth of pink-sheet stocks.

Penny-stock brokers can make a tremendous amount of money in stocks that have large spreads. A major disadvantage of pink-sheet stocks is that typically only one major brokerage firm makes a market in that stock. Consequently, that firm can easily increase the spread and give itself a bigger profit. It is not uncommon for a penny-stock broker to buy 100,000 shares of a pink-sheet stock for $.02 from an investor who wants to sell and then turn around and sell those 100,000 shares for $.06 to an investor who hasn't done his or her homework to check the bid and asked prices. A cost of $.06 a share sounds good and because the investor is buying from a market maker, he or she doesn't even have to pay a commission. Foolish investor! Out of the $6,000 that the investor is paying to buy the shares, $4,000 is profit that will be divided by the broker and the brokerage firm. Only $2,000 actually goes toward purchasing the stock. In addition, because the bid is only $.02, the stock will have to go up 200 percent for the investor to break even!

I believe that the smart investor should buy stocks that are at least listed on the Nasdaq system. This is a computerized system that provides brokers and dealers with the security's price at the touch of a finger when the company's stock symbol is typed into the system. To continue being listed on the Nasdaq system, a company must meet the specific qualifications of having at least $2 million in assets and capital and a surplus of at least $1 million. If a company has a stock symbol and is listed on the Nasdaq system, you know it is a reporting company, which means that it must send its shareholders quarterly and annual reports.

THREE CRITERIA FOR SUCCESSFUL STOCK PICKS

When I decided to specialize in quality, low-priced stocks, I wanted to discover the best way to analyze these stocks to weed out the speculative investments. After years of studying fundamental analysis of blue chip stocks, I have modified those methods of analysis for low-priced stocks. This successful technique for picking bargain stocks contains the following three criteria that a stock should meet to have the most profit potential:

1. The stock should have good sales.
2. The stock should have increased earnings (profits).
3. The stock should be near its 52-week low price.

In the fall of 1991 I recommended Amvestors Financial Corporation (Nasdaq National Market System symbol AVFC) at $1.63 bid. The company had posted a good increase in its second-quarter sales of $41 million, up significantly from $34 million the previous year. The net income was $1.3 million or $.09 per share, compared to $543,000 or $.04 per share a year earlier. In addition, the $1.63 price was near its 52-week low. In about a year Amvestors' stock price had soared to $5.75 or +253 percent!

Increasing sales and earnings show that demand exists for a company's products and that it can cover the additional costs to expand facilities to continue its growth. More importantly, increasing earnings (profits) indicate that the company is successfully marketing its product. Year after year of increasing profits signify that the company has the potential to move from a blue CHEAP stock to a blue chip stock. The low stock price is the most important factor. Because most stocks are cyclical, moving from near their 52-week low to near their 52-week high, it just doesn't make sense to buy them when they are at the high point. I heartily disagree with brokers who call their clients and tell them about a great stock that is setting new price records and recommend that they buy it at the new record price because "it should continue to go higher."

It is not uncommon to analyze a stock and determine that it is a good investment yet decide the stock price is too high. If that's the case, check the stock price occasionally. When it moves down, reexamine the company to make sure that no negative news is causing the stock price to drop. If there isn't any negative news, you have a great investment opportunity—a quality company at a low price.

The previously mentioned three factors are very important to the success of your investment. Having the patience and discipline to wait to purchase that quality stock near its 52-week low should guarantee a potential profit about 80 percent of the time.

LITTLE COMPETITION MEANS VERY HIGH PROFITS

In just about any business environment, a company that offers a good product with little competition will be extremely prosperous. Perhaps one reason I have been so successful recommending quality stocks under $10 is that there is very little Wall Street competition.

Most analysts and brokers with major brokerage firms ignore stocks under $10. The majority of their recommendations are for stocks $15 and over. At the other end of the spectrum, there is a lot of competition in the highly speculative penny stocks and pink-sheet stocks. Investing in quality stocks under $10 is often forgotten and left to the few of us who are smart enough to recognize the potential.

When a good quality stock is at $1 a share, Wall Street usually doesn't get excited about it until it has moved up above $10. One such company was Atari Corporation. In 1993 I recommended Atari at $1.00. This well-known company is a major player in the computer entertainment field. It was selling for one-half of its book value; yet it had good cash assets, a new product line that would shortly be introduced and great profit potential. At that time no one else was interested in the stock. It had to move up to $11 before the major brokerage firms began to recommend it.

Atari eventually hit a high of $12.75. Investors who waited for their brokers to call them with the recommendation at $11 probably got burned, as the stock fell to $6 shortly thereafter. However, if those investors had bought at my $1.00 recommendation, they could have made a 1,175 percent profit! Atari illustrates how the investor can be the big winner by purchasing a quality, low-priced stock before Wall Street becomes interested in it. Atari had already moved up 1,000 percent from my $1.00 recommendation by the time the major Wall Street firms recommended it at $11. It pays to keep your eyes open for good investments.

HOW TO FOLLOW YOUR STOCKS

In Chapter 1 you learned how to read a stock page. Following your stock involves checking the price at least once a week or more if the stock is volatile. There are several ways you can get a price quote. Of course, if the stock is listed in *The Wall Street Journal, Investor's Business Daily* or your local newspaper, you can study it every day. You can call your broker for a price quote, but he or she won't appreciate it if you frequently call when the market is open and prevent your broker from making a commission. Unless you are considering selling the stock, I suggest calling for a quote after the market has closed.

You can also take advantage of a 24-hour telephone quote service offered by many brokers. You usually have to open an account, and you may be required to trade a certain number of times to use the service. Contact your broker to see if his or her firm offers a stock-quote service. However you do it, it is important that you follow the prices of your stocks so you don't miss any opportunities to make a profit.

CHAPTER

7

Mastering New Issues

The goal of many entrepreneurs when forming a company is eventually to take it public by offering shares of its stock to the public. This is the entrepreneur's opportunity to become rich, powerful and well known, and it must be immensely satisfying to open up the morning paper to check the price of *your company*. Part of achieving the American Dream, going public is a great opportunity for the entrepreneur, the company, its employees and its investors.

THE NEW-ISSUE PROCESS

To better understand what you are getting when you purchase a new issue, let's start at the beginning of founding a company to look at the aspects of going public and issuing stock.

Entrepreneur's Dream

Most companies begin with an idea for a new product or service or a better way of offering an existing product or service. The founder (or entrepreneur) establishes the company to fulfill that idea. The founder usually has enough capital or is able to borrow enough from family and friends to get going. However, when additional capital is needed to expand research and development, production or marketing, the company may find itself in the Catch-22 situation of finding that most banks aren't interested in lending money to small companies when they need it. So the company offers a new issue of stock to obtain the needed capital.

The Business Plan

One of the most important documents a company will prepare is its business plan. In essence, the plan is a map that the company intends to follow to successfully bring its product or service to the market. The business plan must have an appreciation of present realities and must indicate a logical course of action, including the capital and resources needed. It should take into account the overall industry, trends, potential problems and economic direction. It should also include company characteristics, its balance sheet, the caliber of its management and specific company goals.

The business plan is vital because it is the first document that any bank, venture-capital firm, investment banker or underwriter will request when a company is seeking to raise capital. Let's assume that King Arthur Winery has achieved good sales and earnings by selling its wine for six years in the Midwest; however, it wants to expand its market to the West Coast. An aggressive expansion of its market will cost King Arthur Winery a tremendous initial investment. The company doesn't have enough capital for the expansion, so it decides to raise the capital through a public offering of a percentage of its stock. This is an important decision, and the advantages and disadvantages of going public should be carefully analyzed.

As explained in Chapter 4, going public is one of the easier ways and sometimes the only way to get needed capital. The public offering puts a value on the company and can be used as an incentive to attract or motivate key personnel. Once the company has public shares, it can use them as collateral when additional capital is needed.

However, offering a new issue does have a negative side: issuing the stock and keeping the shareholders up to date are expensive undertakings. Once public, the company (except for pink-sheet stocks) is obligated to file reports with the SEC, which greatly increases paperwork and legal expenses (as much as $100,000 per year). The company loses privacy, for now the shareholders have a right to know everything that can affect the company's success. It also loses control over some major decisions, such as mergers, and there is increased pressure for better sales and earnings.

Once the King Arthur Winery has carefully weighed both the pros and cons and decides to go public, it must locate a brokerage firm that is willing to underwrite its new-issue stock.

The Underwriter

An *underwriter* is a brokerage firm that acts as the intermediary between the company issuing new securities and the investing public. The underwriter (or investment banker) either by itself or as part of a syndicate (two or more underwriters) agrees to purchase a new issue of securities from a company and distribute it to the investors. A major consideration of the new issue is what percent of the company should be given to the public for the amount of capital the company wants to raise. Let's say that the underwriter and King Arthur Winery decide that it needs to give up 50 percent of the company to raise $3.5 million for the market-expansion program.

The company and the underwriter sign an agreement that represents the underwriter's commitment to purchase the securities, and King Arthur Winery agrees to pay all expenses incurred in preparing the stock issue for resale, including the costs of registration with the SEC and preparing, printing and distributing the prospectus.

Structuring the Deal

The underwriter will determine how much money the company can raise and at what price the shares should sell. Once a value has been given to the new issue, there are many combinations of shares and prices. For example, if $3.5 million is to be raised, it can be offered for several different prices.

Number of Shares	×	Price	=	Amount Raised
350,000		$10.00		$3,500,000
700,000		5.00		3,500,000
1,000,000		3.50		3,500,000
3,500,000		1.00		3,500,000
7,000,000		.50		3,500,000
14,000,000		.25		3,500,000

Number of Shares	×	Price	=	Amount Raised
35,000,000		.10		3,500,000
70,000,000		.05		3,500,000
350,000,000		.01		3,500,000

The underwriter, using expertise gained from previous new-issue offerings, determines the price that it believes will be most advantageous for selling the new issue. The price of the stock then will define how many shares will be offered.

Registering with the Securities and Exchange Commission (SEC)

There are two SEC registration forms: (1) the S-18 is filed by a company raising up to $5 million, and (2) the S-1 is filed when the company intends to raise more than $5 million. Although the SEC is headquartered in Washington, D.C., several SEC offices are located throughout the United States, and a company wanting to file an S-18 or S-1 will send it to the nearest office. An investor who wants to investigate a company or an individual connected with the company can use the SEC library at any of the regional or branch offices. SEC offices are located in Atlanta, Boston, Chicago, Denver, Fort Worth, Los Angeles, Miami, New York, Philadelphia, Salt Lake City, San Francisco, Seattle and Washington, D.C.

Warning: Most investors mistakenly believe that the SEC protects them from new-issue frauds. While the SEC reviews the registration statement of a company, it *does not have the authority* to pass judgment on the worth of the securities of that particular offering.

Many investors assume that if a new issue is registered with the SEC, the SEC checks out the company and gives it an approval. This is a false assumption. The SEC has *no power to prohibit an offering* on the basis that it considers the investment opportunity to be a poor risk. The sole thrust of the federal statute is the disclosure of relevant information. No matter how speculative the investment, no matter how poor the offering, it will comply with federal law if all required facts are disclosed. In essence, as long as a company fills out the registration forms correctly, the SEC must allow the company to sell its securities.

Red Herring

After the registration statement is filed with the SEC, a waiting period begins before the final approval of the registration. The SEC normally takes at least 30 days to review the filing. However, the waiting period could be much longer if the SEC has received many registrations. There usually is a rush of filings at the end of each quarter, which can delay the review.

In the interim the underwriter can give prospective investors the preliminary prospectus or *red herring* (so named for the red ink on the cover page of the brochure). The red herring offers financial details about the issue or statutory prospectus; however, parts of the document may be changed before the final prospectus is issued.

Prospectus

Once the company has satisfied all SEC requirements and made any changes required by the SEC, it can then have the final prospectus printed. This document is supposed to be given to investors before the offer or sale of securities can be made. I recommend that all investors carefully read the prospectus before making a decision on the investment. SEC law states that investors in a new issue must be sent a prospectus and must have time to read it before purchasing the security.

No matter how good the broker makes the company sound, take time to read about it. You may save yourself a lot of money and aggravation.

Filing in Individual States

After the company files its registration form to offer a new issue with the SEC, the underwriter must apply directly to each state in which the underwriter desires to sell shares. Virtually all states have a form of the blue-sky law, which was written to protect the citizens of that state from securities frauds.

The term *blue sky* originated from a famous 1915 case in which Justice McKenna asserted that a particular stock offering had as much value as a "patch of blue sky." The blue-sky law requires sellers of new-stock issues to register their offerings and provide financial details on each issue so investors can base their judgments on relevant data.

However, the blue-sky laws of some states are so restrictive that almost all new issues fail to meet their stringent requirements. How does this affect you? An underwriter cannot legally sell shares of a new issue to an investor unless that investor is a resident of a state in which that new issue is registered. If you live in a state with very restrictive blue-sky laws, it may be virtually impossible for you to invest in any new issue before it goes public.

TYPES OF NEW-ISSUE OFFERINGS

When an underwriter buys a new issue from a company, it must decide how confident it is that the new issue will sell. Based on that confidence, the firm will either underwrite the new issue as a *firm-commitment* or *best-effort* offering.

The best type of new-issue offering is a firm commitment, which means the underwriter is putting its reputation and company on the line. The underwriter is committing to purchase *all* the new-issue securities for sale to its customers. If all the shares are not sold, the underwriter is obligated to pay the company and hold the unsold shares in its own account.

> **Example:**   If an underwriter gives King Arthur Winery a firm commitment for its new-issue offering of 3.5 million shares at $1 each, the underwriter is guaranteeing that the company will receive $3.5 million (minus commissions and expenses) whether it sells all the shares or not.

The second and more speculative type of new-issue offering is called a best-effort offering. This is an agreement between the underwriter and the company that the underwriter will act as an agency to sell the shares, promising to apply its best effort in selling the new issue to its customers. However, no guarantee is given that the offering will succeed. A minimum/maximum number of shares usually is listed in the prospectus.

For the new-issue offering to go through, at least the minimum number of shares must be sold, or all monies will be returned to the investors. This means that the company issuing the securities doesn't get its needed capital and has spent tens of thousands of dollars in legal fees, printing costs, time expended, etc., for nothing. Even though this sounds pretty grim, the vast majority of best-effort new-issue offerings do succeed.

> **Example:** The underwriter has set a minimum of 2 million shares and a maximum of 3.5 million shares at $1 for King Arthur Winery. If the underwriter is able to sell 2 million or more shares, the new issue will go through. If the underwriter is unsuccessful in selling the 2 million minimum, the investors will have their money returned.

When the investor buys new-issue stock from the underwriter, his or her money is put into an escrow account until the new issue actually goes public and starts trading. Because the underwriter has 90 days in which to sell the new issue and can get a 90-day extension, the investor's money can be tied up for six months or more. Why buy from the underwriter then? Because in many cases, the purchase price of the new issue immediately jumps up once it goes public and is offered on the secondary market. In addition, by purchasing a stock from the underwriter at the new-issue price, the investor pays no commission.

UNDERWRITER SYNDICATION AND SUPPORT OF THE NEW ISSUE

In most instances, when an underwriter contracts to take a company public, the syndication department recruits other brokerage firms to take part of the new issue. (See Figure 7.1.)

Working together, the brokers in the selling group market the shares to their customers and, once it goes public, continue to support the new issue with investors who will buy the stock in the aftermarket (the secondary market). Doing so creates an orderly and fair market for the stock.

The selling group continues to promote and support the new issue after it goes public by offering the stock to more customers when the stock is on the secondary market. Because of the number and diversity of the brokerage firms involved, more investors become aware of the stock, and the group of potential investors in the company vastly increases.

That's the scenario I like to see. However, when a new issue is a penny stock with no stock symbol and usually only one underwriter, the scenario changes. (See Figure 7.2.) Because the underwriter does not syndicate the new issue, it can better control the price of the stock.

Figure 7.1   Underwriter Syndication

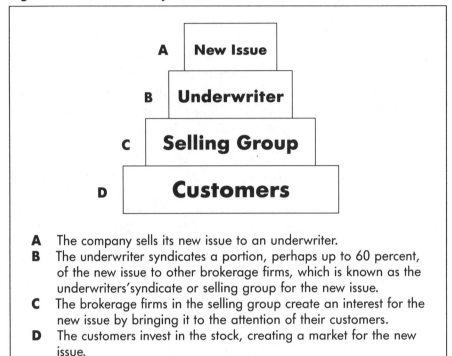

A   The company sells its new issue to an underwriter.
B   The underwriter syndicates a portion, perhaps up to 60 percent, of the new issue to other brokerage firms, which is known as the underwriters'syndicate or selling group for the new issue.
C   The brokerage firms in the selling group create an interest for the new issue by bringing it to the attention of their customers.
D   The customers invest in the stock, creating a market for the new issue.

However, the market has been artificially created, and the stock price may plunge when the underwriter moves on to its next new issue.

Major brokerage firms usually derive a small percentage of their total sales from new issues. However, many penny firms obtain the majority of their total sales from underwriting new issues. The more brokers involved in a new issue, the better the chance for good support of the stock in the aftermarket.

An important new-issue term is *quiet period*. This usually is a 90-day period after the effective date when no new information is allowed to be released about the company. For the purpose of maintaining an orderly aftermarket, the SEC requires the quiet period to regulate public statements by the company.

If the company has some very good news to release during the quiet period, such as a new contract or agreement with a major company, it can petition the SEC for permission to release the information. If the SEC okays the petition, the company can add a sticker to the front page of the prospectus that contains a brief outline

Figure 7.2   Penny-Stock New Issues

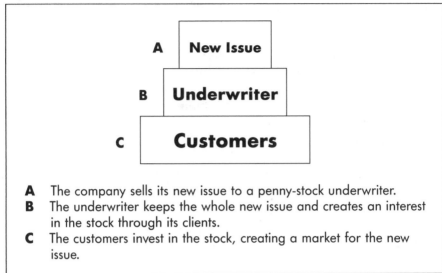

A   The company sells its new issue to a penny-stock underwriter.
B   The underwriter keeps the whole new issue and creates an interest in the stock through its clients.
C   The customers invest in the stock, creating a market for the new issue.

of the news. From the legal point of view, *a broker, newsletter or newspaper can only report information that is included in the prospectus when promoting a company offering a new issue.*

However, this rule is often violated, especially by penny-stock brokers who tell their customers information not contained in the prospectus, such as future plans or a contract or agreement that should be completed in the near future. Sometimes the future plans or contracts do materialize, but often they don't. Believe only what is written in the prospectus, and you won't be disappointed.

HOW TO EASILY READ A NEW-ISSUE PROSPECTUS

Whenever you are looking to purchase a new issue, the *first* step you should take is to read the new-issue prospectus. If a broker calls you with an "unbelievable investment opportunity" in a new issue, don't just take his or her word; insist that the broker send you a prospectus. By law, a broker is not allowed to sell you a new issue before you read the prospectus, but an unscrupulous broker may "forget" that you haven't seen one.

The *prospectus* is a formal, written offer to sell securities. It contains information that a potential investor needs to make an informed investment decision. The prospectus describes the company's business history, operations, its management's background, financial data, pending litigation (if any) and plans, including the use of the proceeds from the new issue.

Once you receive the prospectus, *don't be intimidated by all the legal terminology*. Reading a prospectus, especially for the first time, can be a real chore. Use the highlights that follow to quickly learn what the new issue has to offer, and determine if you want to invest in it. Every prospectus is slightly different, so the items mentioned here may not be found in the prospectus you are reading.

Take a look at our sample prospectus title page for King Arthur Winery in Figure 7.3.

An explanation of sections A through H in Figure 7.3 follows, starting from the top of the page:

- *Section A.* In this section the total number of shares or units (combination of shares plus warrants) that the company is offering for sale to the public is listed.
- *Section B.* This section provides the name of the company that is offering shares or units to the public.
- *Section C.* If the company is offering a unit, this section tells what the unit consists of. It also gives details of the value of the shares and the warrants. It sets the warrant's exercise price and expiration date. (See Chapter 10 on warrants for further details.)
- *Section D.* This statement, an SEC-required summary of the risk factors, is included in *every* prospectus.
- *Section E.* This is a disclaimer that states that the securities have not been approved or disapproved by the SEC. In addition, while the SEC has required that the company follow the correct procedure in filing for the public offering, the SEC is not guaranteeing the accuracy of the information contained in the prospectus. This statement is also included in *every* prospectus. In essence, the SEC does not investigate any new issue to determine if it is a good investment. What the SEC does is to make sure the company "follows the rules" for filing the new issue.
- *Section F.* The table shows the price of the new issue ($1 per unit), the commission the underwriter will receive for selling each unit ($.10) and the actual amount of proceeds the company will receive from each unit ($.90). It also shows the extension of this information for the total offering.
- *Section G.* This is the name and address of the underwriter from which you can purchase the new issue before it goes public. You

Figure 7.3 King Arthur Winery Prospectus

A
B
C

3,500,000 Units
KING ARTHUR WINERY

Each Unit Consisting of One Share of
Common Stock and Two Warrants
to Purchase a Share of Common Stock

King Arthur Winery (the "Company") is hereby offering 3,500,000 units (the "Units"), each Unit consisting of one share of the Company's common stock, $.01 par value (the Common Stock") and two Common Stock Purchase Warrants (the "Warrants"). The Common Stock and the Warrants will be separately transferable immediately after the date of this Prospectus. Each Warrant entitles the holder to purchase one share of Common Stock at a price equal to the initial offering price of the Units commencing on January 6, 1996. The Warrants expire two years from the date of this Prospectus and are redeemable upon 45 days' written notice by the Company at $0.50 per Warrant beginning 30 days after they become exercisable. For more detailed information regarding the Warrants, see "Description of Securities."

The initial public offering price per Unit will be $1.00. Prior to this offering (the "Offering"), there has been no public market for the Units, the Common Stock, or the Warrants. There is no assurance that an active trading market will develop or be maintained following the Offering. The initial public offering price of the Units and the terms of the Warrants were determined by negotiation between the Company and W. K. Mathews Securities, Inc., the representative (the "Representative") of the several underwriters of the Offering (the "Underwriters"). See "Underwriting."

D   THE SECURITIES OFFERED HEREBY INVOLVE A HIGH DEGREE
OF RISK AND THEIR PURCHASE SHOULD BE CONSIDERED ONLY
BY PERSONS ABLE TO SUSTAIN A TOTAL LOSS OF THEIR
INVESTMENT. SEE "RISK FACTORS."

E   THESE SECURITIES HAVE NOT BEEN APPROVED OR
DISAPPROVED BY THE SECURITIES AND EXCHANGE
COMMISSION, NOR HAS THE COMMISSION PASSED UPON THE
ACCURACY OR ADEQUACY OF THIS PROSPECTUS. ANY
REPRESENTATION TO THE CONTRARY IS A CRIMINAL OFFENSE.

F

	Price to Public	Underwriting Discounts and Commissions	Proceeds to Company
Per Unit	$1.00	$ .10	$ .90
Total	$3,500,000	$350,000	$3,150,000

G   W. K. MATHEWS SECURITIES, INC.
1000 N. MICHIGAN AVE.
CHICAGO, IL 60601

H   The date of this Prospectus is January 6, 1994

can purchase the new issue only from that underwriter or other members in the syndicate of underwriters that are bringing the company public. Once the new issue goes public, you can purchase the stock from any broker.

- *Section H.* This section shows the effective date (the date when a registered offering may be sold to the public). The underwriter normally has 90 days from the effective date to sell the new issue. If the underwriter runs into difficulties selling the security, it may obtain a 90-day extension to complete the offering.

The first page of the prospectus tells quite a bit about the cost of the new-issue security and where you can purchase it. Inside the prospectus, you will learn about the company, its products or services, its goals, its marketplace and competition, the quality of its management and other factors important to the success of the new issue.

After checking the first page of the prospectus, turn to the prospectus summary (usually near the front of the prospectus). The summary outlines the most important information in the prospectus. It contains information about the following:

- *The Company.* This section details the company's background, business and products or services offered.
- *The Offering.* The offering section explains the number of shares or units being sold. If units are involved, it specifies what each unit comprises. If warrants are involved in the offering, the exercise price and expiration date are stipulated.
- *Shares Outstanding after the Offering.* This part tells the total amount of shares outstanding, including the new issue. To determine what percentage of the company is being given to the public, divide the number of shares offered by the total number of shares outstanding. I like to see a company give 35 to 60 percent of its ownership in a public offering.

    Example: If King Arthur Winery has 7 million total shares outstanding and the offering is 3.5 million, the winery is offering 50 percent of its company to the public.

- *Use of Proceeds.* This explains in detail how the company plans to spend the money raised by the new issue. Many times the proceeds are used to pay off long-term debt, for the development of new products or as working capital. Look for a specific plan to expand the company's product or service or, in the case of a company in the development stage, to bring its product to the market. The plan should state the amount of money to be spent at a specific time to implement the various stages of the strategy. If the prospectus is vague about how the capital will be utilized, *stay away* from that new issue.

Hint: Avoid any new issue that plans to use the proceeds to repay loans from the management. The new issue is being used to benefit the company's management rather than the company itself.

- *Proposed Nasdaq Symbol.* This is the company's stock symbol that will be used when the stock starts to trade. A smart company will plan ahead and obtain its Nasdaq stock symbol so that when it goes public, it can immediately be listed on the Nasdaq system. Many companies will try to select a stock symbol that relates to its business. For example, King Arthur Winery may choose the stock symbol WINE.
- *Selected Financial Information.* This section lists information about the company's finances. It usually includes sales or revenues, net income and net income per share for the past three or more years. This section should also give the total assets, total current assets, total current liabilities and shareholder's equity.

By reading the prospectus summary, you should be able to decide if the company has a good chance of being successful. If after reading the summary, you still believe it is a good potential investment, you will want to check further by reading selected areas in the rest of the prospectus. Make sure that you read about these areas:

- *The Management.* Review the management's background to see if these people possess the necessary experience and knowledge to be an asset to the company. If their background experience is in completely different areas from the company's business, *be very careful.* Check whether the chairperson of the board, president and vice president are spending 100 percent of their time with the company. If key management personnel are not devoting themselves solely to that company, *stay away.* If they have headed one or more public companies that ended up in bankruptcy, *do not invest.*
- *Litigation.* Be sure that the company is not involved in any major lawsuits that could seriously affect its business.
- *Management Compensation.* This can help the potential investor determine if the management is weakening the company with huge

salaries. I would rather see salaries below average with bonus incentives paid when management achieves certain goals regarding increasing sales and earnings.

- *Risk Factors.* The prospectus is filled with bleak and discouraging disclaimers that are required by the SEC. While the SEC is trying to protect potential investors by making sure that they understand all the risks involved in buying a new issue, it can frighten an investor away from a good investment. Once you have read a few prospectuses, you will recognize the disclaimers and take them into consideration without letting them discourage you from investing in a quality new issue.

MAKING AND LOSING MONEY IN NEW ISSUES

New-issue securities can offer great profit potential if the investor checks before investing. Many poor new-issue investments can be eliminated just by carefully reading the prospectus. Buy a new issue only *at the new-issue price;* otherwise, you may end up paying an inflated price. This is a key factor that can determine whether or not you make a good profit. In many cases, once the new issue goes public and is allowed to trade on the secondary market, the price skyrockets. Investors who were unable to purchase a stock at $1 at the new-issue price may find themselves paying $2 for the same stock once it goes public.

Be aware that many new issues are very overpriced. Analyze the company as you would any other stock and purchase the new issue only if you would buy it at that price if it were a common stock. Avoid new issues that do not raise at least $4 million. Even if the new issue is a company in the development stage, the $4 million will guarantee the stock a listing on Nasdaq. Always make sure the new issue will be listed at least on the Nasdaq system. If the company plans merely to be listed on the pink sheets or the Vancouver Stock Exchange, *do not invest in it.*

The state in which you reside will determine whether or not you can purchase a new issue. Several states have relaxed blue-sky laws, allowing investors to purchase most new issues, including Colorado, Florida, Illinois, Nevada, New Jersey, New York and Utah. Some states are very restrictive about new issues. It is virtually impossible to purchase a new issue if you reside in California, Pennsylvania, Texas or Wisconsin. Since blue-sky laws continue to change, you can check out your state's laws by contacting your local state securities department, which is usually located in the state capital.

I believe that the restrictive states are making a mistake. While protecting investors from poor investments, these states also keep investors from buying some great low-priced stocks. Often a $1 new issue will not meet the criteria of those states, and their citizens will be unable to purchase the new issue before it goes public. Once the stock has gone public and received the capital raised by the stock issue, it then qualifies for listing in Standard & Poor's, which automatically allows the stock to be bought by residents in most states. However, by that time the stock price has already jumped from the $1 new-issue price to $1.75, $2 or higher. I have recommended many new issues over the years that have been great investments. One of my superstars is CarePlus, a $1 new issue that went public in December 1983. CarePlus provides home health care, catering to the acutely ill patient. The company offers many services, from laboratory tests, pharmaceuticals, nutritional feeding through a vein or tube to anticancer drug administration, intravenous organic drug administration and rehabilitation therapy. At the time I recommended CarePlus I believed that home health care would expand tremendously, since it is much cheaper than hospitalization. The company didn't disappoint me. In January 1991 it traded at $22, which gave my subscribers a nice 2,100 percent return.

Once you have determined that a new issue is a good investment (i.e., a quality company at a low price) and have purchased the new issue, it is essential that you monitor your stock very carefully. Many times a new issue will skyrocket and then just as quickly fall back. If you get a good profit (30 to 50 percent), *don't be afraid to take that profit.*

CHAPTER

8

Mastering Stocks
in Bankruptcy

One investment area that has been almost universally ignored by the media is investing in companies in bankruptcy. Perhaps the reason is that the term *bankruptcy* is so negative that most investors, brokerage firms and analysts don't even consider a company in bankruptcy as an investment. There has been insufficient research on companies in bankruptcy, and very little information is readily available for the average investor.

While they are speculative, companies in bankruptcy can offer great investment potential. If you are confused about the bankruptcy process, don't feel lonely. To the average person, bankruptcy means liquidating all of a company's assets and going out of business. Bankruptcy can mean that; however, Chapter 11 of the Bankruptcy Law offers an alternative to liquidation through the reorganization of the company. Sure, the company has major problems, but under Chapter 11 it is protected from its creditors while it reorganizes and conducts business, and it may very well survive that difficult period of time.

In fact, a company that experienced one of the largest percentage gains during the 1980s was Envirodyne Industries, a Chicago company that was selling for $.25 in 1981 when it was in Chapter 11. It successfully reorganized under Chapter 11 and was bought out for $80 per share (taking into consideration a two-for-one stock split).

Figure 8.1   Chapter 11 Companies

Successes	Failures
Chicago-Milwaukee Railroad	Diamond Reo Motors
Envirodyne Industries	E. J. Korvettes
Storage Technology	Osborne Computer
Toys R Us	Sambo's Restaurants
Wickes Companies, Inc.	W. T. Grant Company

That's an incredible gain of almost 319 times the original $.25 investment!

The CHEAP Investor didn't do quite that well, for the newsletter recommended Envirodyne in October 1984 when it was at $2.81. When Envirodyne was bought out at $80 by the former management group of Beatrice, my subscribers had a potential profit of 2,747 percent! Five other Chapter 11 companies that increased by several hundred percent from their original *CHEAP Investor* recommendation prices are Charter Company, Storage Technology, AM International, Lionel Corporation and Wickes Companies.

The potential is there; the investor just needs to understand the bankruptcy process and how to analyze companies in Chapter 11. Investors can make quite a profit by investing in companies in Chapter 11 because as soon as Wall Street hears the rumor that a company is on the verge of entering Chapter 11, it panics. The stock price plunges as everyone bails out, and many times the price falls well below the true value of the company. After carefully analyzing the company to determine if it will be a survivor, the smart investor doesn't let this opportunity escape. He or she can purchase stock worth much more for just a fraction of the price that investors were recently paying for it.

Many companies have reorganized under Chapter 11 and emerged to become prosperous, vital enterprises. On the other side of the coin, not every company survives Chapter 11. Sometimes there are just too many negative factors, and after all is said and done, the company still goes into liquidation.

The list in Figure 8.1 shows companies that succeeded or failed in Chapter 11. Some of the failures are well-known names. That is why it is imperative to understand the bankruptcy process and thoroughly analyze the company *before* you invest.

BANKRUPTCY (CHAPTER 11): AN OVERVIEW

To fully understand Chapter 11, you must first learn what bankruptcy encompasses. Bankruptcy is defined as "the state of insolvency of a person or corporation." Very simply, it is the inability of a person or company to pay its debts. The Bankruptcy Law was designed to accomplish two main objectives: (1) to protect the debtor (company filing bankruptcy) against any frivolous suits by creditors (companies or individuals who are owed money), especially when the debtor is still able to recover; and (2) to provide a fair means for distribution of a debtor's assets among all creditors. The bankruptcy process establishes priorities among creditors and prohibits the debtor from favoring one creditor over another.

The bankruptcy code contains several chapters. However, Chapter 7 and Chapter 11 are the only two that companies can use. Companies that suffer severe financial difficulties have a choice of liquidating (Chapter 7) or reorganizing (Chapter 11). Chapter 7 means selling all the company's assets and distributing the monies received from the sale to creditors. The big disadvantage of Chapter 7 for the creditors is that they usually receive only a small percentage of the money owed them. Common shareholders may receive only a few cents per dollar value of the share.

The *best* alternative to liquidation for a company and its creditors and shareholders is filing for Chapter 11 to restructure the company's debts in the hope that it can reorganize and prosper. Chapter 11 is the financial restructuring of a company after it has filed for protection from its creditors while it works out a plan to repay its overdue debt. The company normally files a reorganization plan within 120 days, and its debts are usually frozen for up to three years until the plan is approved. The aim of reorganization is to allow the company to continue operations while it negotiates with creditors and to eventually return the company to financial health.

If the plan does not work, the company may be liquidated (Chapter 7) and its assets sold to pay the claims of creditors and shareholders. However, if the company succeeds, the creditors should be able to get most of the money owed them. In many cases creditors have been very pleased with the settlements from large companies that have entered Chapter 11.

LOCATING COMPANIES IN CHAPTER 11

In general, the easiest way to find companies in Chapter 11 is to read the stock tables in your local newspaper, *The Wall Street Journal, Investor's Business Daily* or *Barron's*.

The vast majority of NYSE and AMEX stock tables designate a Chapter 11 company by putting the letters *vj* before the stock name. However, *Investor's Business Daily* uses a *b* to designate a company in Chapter 11. If you also want to check the Nasdaq stocks, companies in Chapter 11 are indicated with a *q*.

If you look at a list of companies that shows only the stock symbols, you can still tell which companies are in Chapter 11. When a company files for Chapter 11, its stock symbol normally is changed by adding a *Q* before the symbol. By investing just 15 or 20 minutes in scanning the stock pages, you can gather a pretty good list of Chapter 11 companies. A list of some NYSE companies currently in bankruptcy is shown in Figure 8.2.

CHARACTERISTICS OF CHAPTER 11 SURVIVORS

Now that you have compiled a list of companies in Chapter 11, the next step is to obtain information about them so you can determine which ones may be good investments. Sometimes information on Chapter 11 companies can be extremely difficult to find. Contacting the company and requesting the annual and quarterly reports can provide good background information. Another great informational source is a copy of the reorganization plan that the company usually issues within three to six months after filing for Chapter 11. The plan can be requested by calling or writing the company. However, many Chapter 11 companies require a $50 to $100 fee for a copy of the reorganization plan (even if you are a shareholder). Therefore, eliminate any companies that do not have good investment potential before paying $50 or more for the plan.

Certain types of companies have generally proven to be good investments when they emerge from Chapter 11. There are always exceptions to the rule, but by looking for the following fundamentals, you can pare your list to a more manageable number of companies for in-depth research.

Figure 8.2   Major Companies Currently in Chapter 11

Company Name	Stock Symbol	All-Time High Price	52-Week High	52-Week Low	Last
vjAileen, Inc.	AEE	$29.50	$ 7.75	$ 1.38	$ 1.75
vjColumbia Gas System	CG	$56.50	$27.50	$19.75	$24.75
vjContl Information Sys	CNY	$13.63	$ .30	$ .05	$ .09
vjCrystal Brands	CBR	$37.88	$ 3.63	$ .38	$ .44
vjJamesway Corporation	JMY	$16.25	$ 3.38	$ .03	$ .75
vjLeslie Fay Cos	LES	$23.13	$12.00	$ 2.63	$ 3.38
vjLiberte Investors	LBI	$35.88	$ 2.63	$ .50	$ 2.00
vjLone Star Industries	LCE	$41.75	$ 2.75	$ 1.38	$ 2.38
vjMerry-Go-Round Ent.	MGR	$22.00	$17.63	$ 1.38	$ 3.00

Companies with Huge Sales

Experience has taught me that the best type of Chapter 11 company is one with annual sales of at least $300 million. Any time a company enters Chapter 11, there is a chance that it will fail and be liquidated. However, a company with sales over $300 million obviously has been around for a while and usually has built up huge assets. It has a greater chance of surviving because the easiest and quickest way for a company to get turned around is to sell off some assets to obtain the necessary capital to continue operations and/or to pay creditors.

On the other hand, a company that has only $50 million in sales and a $40-million debt, for example, is going to be hard-pressed to reorganize, pay its debts and still have enough capital left to operate the company. It is possible but not as likely to happen. The investor should definitely stay away from a company that has more debts than sales. The chances that a company with sales of $400 million and a debt of $900 million will survive are practically nil.

Companies Listed on the NYSE

The New York Stock Exchange (NYSE) has the most stringent requirements for membership. If a company has been successful in the past (which a listing on the NYSE indicates), the chances are greater that it will have the ability and resources to be successful again. NYSE-listed stocks tend to have sales in excess of $300 million and are generally well known on Wall Street, which are tremendous assets.

Often a company on the NYSE will be delisted when it enters Chapter 11, so do some research to discover if it was originally listed on that exchange. (Checking a copy of *The Wall Street Journal* from a month or so prior to the company's entering Chapter 11 should show whether or not it was on the NYSE.)

Companies That Are Former "Darlings" of Wall Street

Another good candidate for successful reorganization under Chapter 11 is a former "darling" or Wall Street favorite. Many companies that had a stock price of $40 or $50 or more and were listed on the NYSE are great investment choices because they are already well known.

Another advantage of a former Wall Street darling is that in most cases, some brokers will continue to trade in the stock. Therefore, the company will have at least a limited following that should help push the price upward when it emerges from Chapter 11. Companies that did not interest Wall Street before they entered Chapter 11 probably would be unable to generate much excitement when they emerge from it.

One Wall Street darling was Storage Technology. The stock that sold as high as $40.38 was a leader in the computer data storage industry. A few years later the company filed for Chapter 11 and traded as low as $1. When the stock emerged from Chapter 11, it sold as low as $2 but quickly jumped to the $7 level because of its Wall Street following and its history of previous success. Currently the stock is selling for about $30.

Companies with Widely Known Names or Products

The most difficult hurdle for a new company is becoming known to the public and Wall Street. A company that does not have a known product has an extra deterrent to surviving reorganization because it still has to sell its product. If a company's product is well known, that asset could make the difference between reorganization and liquidation.

Lionel Corporation is an excellent example. I recommended Lionel in May 1983 at $3.25 when it was ready to come out of Chapter 11. Less than two years later the stock was $14. Lionel's biggest asset was its name recognition. Almost everyone either had a Lionel train when they were growing up or knew someone who did. Once Lionel streamlined its operations and sold off unprofitable divisions, its product sales were enough to ensure the company's success at that time.

SELECTING BANKRUPTCIES WITH THE MOST POTENTIAL

Once you have eliminated the obviously poor Chapter 11 candidates, there are still several areas to check to find the company with the best chances of survival.

Companies That Change Management

Poor management has caused the downfall of many companies. No matter how good a company's products, if they are not marketed effectively and the company is not run efficiently, it will eventually lose money and may be forced into Chapter 11. If the balance sheet is not turned around, the company will be forced to liquidate to pay its debts.

Hiring a new CEO, who often brings his or her own management team, can be an important factor in the survival of a company. There are teams that specialize in turning around companies in or near Chapter 11, and if the team has a record of successfully reorganizing other companies, that's a big bonus. Because the new CEO brings his or her own people, this destroys all the old political alliances and allows the new team to measure products, divisions and employees on performance instead of clout. The ability to impartially cut out the deadwood and sell unprofitable assets is imperative to a company's survival.

Another consideration is the way the new management team is compensated for its work. If the team is paid a small salary but receives a large bonus and/or stock incentives for positive results, it will strive harder to turn the company around. This is because the team has a piece of the action and is being paid in direct proportion to the well-being of the company.

Companies That Become Profitable

A major criterion for successful investment in a Chapter 11 company is to follow the company's income statement until it shows a profit. Even if a company has several of the previously mentioned criteria going for it, its chances of surviving are very slim if it does not recover enough to show a profit. It is imperative to analyze the company's current income statement, which you can find in its latest quarterly report. Take a look at the example in Figure 8.3.

Before we analyze the turnaround of a company's income statement, we need to explain a few terms.

Sales (or Revenues)   This is the monetary payment received in exchange for goods or services or from other sources such as rents, investments, etc. Don't be too concerned about a decrease in sales. In most cases unprofitable subsidiaries have been sold, and this would cause the sales to decline.

Income Continuing Operations   This is one of the most important areas to check on a Chapter 11 company's income statement. It is vital because these operations have survived and will become the basis for the company's sales and earnings. Check the figures to determine whether or not the continuing operations have increased their income over the previous year. An increase is a positive sign that a company is on the road to recovery.

Income Discontinued Operations   This nonrecurring item is shown on the income statement for writing off a product or division that is being discontinued. (Sometimes it is found under "extraordinary item." See below.)

Extraordinary Item Tax Credit   This nonrecurring credit offers a direct dollar-for-dollar reduction in tax liability. When a company loses money, that loss becomes a positive factor once the company becomes profitable again because the loss is deducted from taxable income and the company pays less tax.

> **Example:**   Chrysler at one time experienced tremendous losses. When Lee Iacocca turned the company around and it became profitable, those losses came back on the income statement as a tax credit (or tax loss carryforward) and were deducted from taxable income. Approximately 30 to 50 per-

Figure 8.3   Sample of a Current Income Statement

	1994	1993
Sales	$4,872,000	$7,950,000
Income Continuing Operations	371,000	(820,000)
Income Discontinued Operations	716,000	(513,000)
Extraordinary Item Tax Credit	394,000	—
Net Income (Loss)	1,481,000	(1,333,000)
Income Continuing Operations per Share	.02	(.05)
Income Discontinued Operations per Share	.04	(.03)
Extraordinary Item per Share	.02	—
Net Income (Loss) per Share	.09	(.08)
Shares Outstanding	16,652,551	16,510,741

cent of Chrysler's net income resulted from the tax credits. Therefore, a large amount of tax credits (losses) can be a big asset to a profitable company.

Net Income or Loss   The finai profit or loss after all costs, expenses and taxes have been deducted, net income may be misleading because it may contain profits from the sale of divisions or tax credits.

Per Share   Per-share items are determined by dividing the continuing operations, net income, etc., by the number of shares outstanding.

Shares Outstanding   This is the total number of shares that have been issued. When comparing net income per share or income continuing operations per share with the previous year's figures, always make sure the shares-outstanding figure is approximately the same. Otherwise, comparing the per-share figures from one period to the next will be of little value.

Many times companies in Chapter 11 will satisfy part of their debts by issuing more common shares. In Figure 8.3 the number of shares is just about the same. However, if the company had issued 30 million shares more to satisfy its debt (which is not uncommon for a Chapter 11 company), then the per-share comparisons would be misleading. (See Figure 8.4.)

Figure 8.4   Income Statement after Issuing a Large Number of Shares

	1994	1993
Sales	$4,872,000	$7,950,000
Income Continuing Operations	371,000	(820,000)
Income Discontinued Operations	716,000	(513,000)
Extraordinary Item Tax Credit	394,000	—
Net Income (Loss)	1,481,000	(1,333,000)
Income Continuing Operations per Share	.01	(.05)
Income Discontinued Operations per Share	.02	(.03)
Extraordinary Item per Share	.01	—
Net Income (Loss) per Share	.03	(.08)
Shares Outstanding	46,652,551	16,510,741

Note that the per-share items for 1994 have dropped drastically from Figure 8.3. By issuing such a large number of shares, the company has greatly diluted the value of its current shares. Dilution of share value should be considered when analyzing any investment.

Companies That Enter a Prepackaged Chapter 11

Recently I have noted a trend toward a prepackaged Chapter 11 filing which is usually positive for a company. This strategy generally is used by a company that has run short of cash. The company negotiates with its major creditors and/or lenders to design a reorganization plan before entering Chapter 11. This type of Chapter 11 filing is successful because the company is generally sound with reasonable debt but lacks an adequate line of credit to continue its business. Filing Chapter 11 gives the company breathing room and the cash infusion it needs to turn itself around.

NYSE-listed Jamesway Corporation, which operates a chain of over 100 discount department stores in the East, is a good example. Jamesway's problem wasn't debt. In fact, in February 1993 it renegotiated its bank debt to extend a line of credit through 1996 to remodel its stores. Jamesway ran into problems when it ran short of cash to pay its suppliers for merchandise to stock the stores. Suppliers stopped shipping, and Jamesway entered a Catch-22 situation. As it wasn't able to obtain as much merchandise to sell, it had even less money to restock its shelves. The company was in a spiral that it had to escape, or it would die.

Jamesway negotiated a $75 million unsecured debtor-in-possession financing plan with CIT Group/Business Credit Corp. In July 1993 the company entered Chapter 11 and received the line of credit that would ensure the cash that Jamesway needed to restock. I analyzed Jamesway's situation and saw the filing of Chapter 11 to be a positive factor. I recommended it at the $.56 to $.63 level. The stock zoomed up to $1.38 in two weeks.

Companies with a Confirmed Reorganization Plan

The strategy to satisfy the creditors of a company in Chapter 11 is called the *reorganization plan*. It usually is a compromise between the Chapter 11 company and the creditors and may involve full or partial payment of debts in cash, securities or other financial incentives.

It is important to read the reorganization plan to determine if a company intends to issue many more shares of its securities to pay off its debts. If so, those new shares will dilute the value of the stock, and the company may decide to use a reverse stock split as a "quick fix" to increase the stock price. I believe that a reverse stock split is very hazardous to the shareholders' wealth. Do not invest in a company that is planning to execute a reverse stock split. If you already own stock, consider selling it.

A company usually files a reorganization plan about 120 days after going into Chapter 11 and normally has to amend it at least a few times over the next two to three years. The goal is to confirm the plan of reorganization, which means that two-thirds of the creditors and a majority of the claims in a class agree to the plan. If the bankruptcy judge approves the confirmed plan of reorganization, the plan binds all creditors, and the company can emerge from bankruptcy.

During reorganization the debtor and representatives for the creditors have periodic meetings. Each creditor representative tries to increase the amount of distribution that his or her group will receive, while the debtor tries to encourage a plan that will allow it to emerge as a successful, reorganized company with adequate funds to continue operations. Needless to say, a lot of discussing and compromising occurs before any plan is confirmed. If no agreement can be reached, the company may still end up in liquidation.

A Chapter 11 company that has a confirmed plan of reorganization has passed a very important hurdle. The time element is important, too. One of the biggest mistakes a company can make is to come out of Chapter 11 too soon. Most successful companies stay in Chapter 11 for around three years to take full advantage of the reorganization period.

I have noticed that some companies in Chapter 11 experience a quick price jump when the reorganization plan is approved. For example, Johns Mansville was selling for around $2, and when the reorganization plan was approved, the stock jumped by about 70 percent during the next week.

NEW TRENDS IN BANKRUPTCIES

Because the public has become so willing to sue over just about anything and the courts are awarding huge settlements, many companies are finding themselves in dire financial straits because of lawsuits resulting from marketing a defective product or a product found to cause problems that show up years after it was used. This attitude has caused some companies to seek the protection from creditors offered by Chapter 11 even though, according to their income statements, they don't really need to be reorganized.

One company that sought protection under Chapter 11 because of massive lawsuits and settlements was A. H. Robbins. Based in Richmond, Virginia, A. H. Robbins is a leading pharmaceutical company. It also is the manufacturer of the Dalkon shield, an intrauterine device (IUD) that has been shown to cause infections and other injuries. Even though the Dalkon shield was pulled from the U.S. market more than 14 years ago, burgeoning lawsuits from women who were injured by the intrauterine birth-control device forced the company to file Chapter 11. When Robbins filed Chapter 11 on August 21, 1985, there were more than 15,500 lawsuits and claims against it from use of the IUD.

Extremely high wages from labor contracts have been attacked by creative use of Chapter 11. Continental Airlines filed for Chapter 11 in the mid-1980s, when its costs became too high to compete in its marketplace. By filing Chapter 11, the company no longer was required to honor contracts, including those with labor unions. Many unions consider this tactic to be union busting. However, it allowed the company to renegotiate lower wages for its employees. In return, the employees were able to keep their jobs instead of having to seek new ones because the business was forced to liquidate. It is ironic that after Continental cut its labor costs (in addition to many other cuts), it not only survived bankruptcy but became a profitable major airline for several years until it again filed Chapter 11 in November 1990.

A. H. Robbins and Continental employed the Chapter 11 laws for reasons other than the original intentions, which shows how changing times can affect the way legislation is utilized. I am not taking sides on whether these companies have stretched the protection of Chapter 11 too far. I do think it is interesting to see companies making use of Chapter 11 in their fight for survival, and I foresee more companies utilizing Chapter 11 for a variety of reasons besides the original intent. Those companies should be treated like any other potential Chapter 11 investment and must be carefully researched.

Management Sellout to Creditors

A disturbing new trend in bankruptcies is the management sellout to its creditors. Chapter 11 was instituted to protect a company from its creditors while it negotiated its debt and tried to successfully reorganize. Smart management teams utilize Chapter 11's protection and the threat of liquidation to negotiate the debt down to $.20 to $.30 on the dollar. This strategy protects the shareholder's equity and allows the company to emerge from reorganization with more assets.

Recently, however, some management-team members seem to be more concerned with satisfying creditors to avoid liquidation and losing their jobs rather than safeguarding the shareholder's investment value and the company's health. Instead of negotiating to reduce the debt, occasionally they will actually pay off the whole debt and give interest to the creditors. The only way they can accomplish this is to offer the creditors shares in the company, which means issuing millions of new shares. This severely dilutes the stock value and shareholder's equity. In many cases the original shareholders may end up with less than 5 percent of the newly restructured company. If you see this happening to a stock you own, *sell it immediately*.

The Shafting of Common Shareholders

Chapter 11 is also being used another way to shaft common shareholders. In some instances, when the company is reorganized, new stock is issued to only the creditors and management. Meanwhile the common shareholders are left out in the cold because they are unsecured creditors. This tactic has been used by Continental Airlines, Continental Bank, Ames Department Stores, Wang Labs and Emerson Radio.

My own experience with this devious method of getting rid of debt was with Emerson Radio. I recommended the stock numerous times over the years, and my subscribers made some good profits. Emerson, a major distributor of electronic equipment, underwent a power struggle in 1992, and a new management group took over.

My last recommendation was in May 1993, when Emerson announced it had reached an agreement in principle to restructure its $225 million outstanding debt. With $800 million in annual sales, this debt wasn't unusual. The stock moved up from $.75 to $1.38 as we waited for the debt restructuring agreement to be signed. (When a definitive agreement is signed, the stock usually soars.)

Instead of signing the agreement with its lenders, the company borrowed from its largest shareholder. It decided to enter Chapter 11, buy back its debt from its creditors at $.30 on the dollar and form a new, restructured company issuing new stock. Unfortunately, new shares weren't issued to common shareholders. Those shareholders saw their investment plunge as the stock became worthless, and most lost their entire investment.

As of this writing, Emerson plans to offer old common shareholders the chance to buy rights for up to 30 percent of the reorganized company's stock. However, I believe that Emerson common shareholders will be quite hesitant to invest in the new stock. If the company had no reservations about shafting the old common shareholders, what's to keep it from pulling the same trick in the future? Run, don't walk from companies like that.

CHAPTER

9

Mastering Turnaround Stocks

I greatly admire John Templeton, the grandfather of modern turnaround (or contrary) investing. In 1939, just after World War II started, Templeton called his broker and gave him a very unusual buy order. He instructed his broker to buy 100 shares of every stock on the NYSE and AMEX that was selling for $1 or less. When the broker called back to confirm that he had bought all the stocks that were $1 or under, he mentioned that of course he didn't buy any stocks that were bankrupt. Templeton startled his broker by insisting that he also purchase the bankrupt stocks that were under $1.

In all, Templeton bought 105 stocks, 35 of which were bankrupt. After about four years, he sold those stocks for more than $40,000 or almost four times his original investment. Why did he buy the stocks? Templeton believed that the United States would eventually enter World War II and that would spur the economy and cause his 105 stocks to appreciate in value. The stocks were extremely cheap, yet the companies had to be of high quality to meet the listing requirements for the NYSE and AMEX. Templeton correctly assumed those stocks had good potential to turn around. Because of their low stock prices, they could easily have greater percentage moves, which would far outpace the higher-priced stocks.

While I certainly don't recommend doing what he did, John Templeton became the most famous and successful money manager in the world. His Templeton Growth Fund is one of the most profitable of all time. Today more than 60 mutual funds bear his name with in excess of $28 billion under management.

One goal that all stock investors share is to find a stock with the potential to be the next Xerox or General Motors. This is a fine goal, though most investors will never achieve it. However, there is one investment area that can provide great profit and self-satisfaction—turnaround stocks.

WHAT IS A TURNAROUND STOCK?

A formerly high-priced, successful stock that has experienced hard times causing a drastic plunge in its stock price meets the first qualification for a turnaround candidate. However, as the name indicates, it also needs to overcome its severe problems and show potential to resume being a successful company. Companies that survive bankruptcy are considered turnaround stocks, but many companies can be turnaround stocks without entering bankruptcy.

Typically, a turnaround stock is promoted to an unrealistically high price with the expectation of higher profits due perhaps to a new product, service or acquisition. When it becomes apparent that the profits have not materialized or that the new acquisition, product or whatever is not going to be as successful as predicted, the stock price takes a nosedive. The price keeps falling, eventually becoming only a fraction of its high price. While the stock was very overpriced at its high, it may be extremely underpriced at its low.

Arrow Electronics—A Turnaround Stock

A company can also experience plummeting stock prices if it generates poor sales and earnings compared to previous quarters. Arrow Electronics on the NYSE is a good example. Its stock quickly soared to more than $35 a share in the mid-1980s as it became a favorite of Wall Street and was on the buy list of virtually every brokerage firm. The stock was promoted by Wall Street to the point that it was extremely overpriced compared to the company's actual value. When Arrow posted some huge losses, the stock price dropped like a rock. As the losses continued, so did the falling price until the stock hit a low of $3.75. Just as Arrow was tremendously overpriced at $35, it was immensely underpriced at $3.75.

In September 1990 I analyzed Arrow and despite large losses, I recommended it because I realized that it had the potential to far outpace the Dow Jones Industrials. Over the next three years the stock not only turned itself around, but its investors must have been extremely gratified to see it soar from the $3.75 level to more than $43, for a 1,047 percent increase! An investment of $3,750 for 1,000 shares would have skyrocketed to $43,000!

It is interesting to note that Arrow was on the buy list of virtually every Wall Street brokerage firm when it was at $35. However, no one wanted it at $3.75 as it was considered a bad investment. The stock price had to really move up before it was again included on the majority of the brokerage firms' buy lists. Of course, by the time the stock hit $43, everyone wanted to buy it.

THE HUGE PROFIT POTENTIAL OF TURNAROUNDS

A quality turnaround stock has the potential to soar. One major advantage of a turnaround stock compared to other low-priced stocks is that it was previously at a much higher price and many analysts already know the stock. Name recognition (for either the company or its products) can make it easier for the stock to move up a second time.

As explained in Chapter 8 on stocks in bankruptcy, panic causes the stock price to continue to drop to the point that it is very undervalued. Recognizing that the company has learned from its errors and has reorganized to solve its previous problems, the investor can purchase the stock for a fraction of its true worth.

Acclaim Entertainment, a video game manufacturer, is a good example of a turnaround stock. Acclaim grew tremendously fast and was on the buy lists of most Wall Street firms when it sold at the $16 level in the late 1980s. The company experienced some hard times in 1990, and the stock plunged to the $3 level in early 1991. I recommended the stock at $3.13 because it was tremendously undervalued and the company was reorganizing to turn itself around. The potential was there, and Acclaim grabbed it to become a major player in the video game/entertainment industry. The stock was again on the buy list as it shot up to $33 per share. In typical Wall Street logic, Acclaim Entertainment was a "sell" at the $3 to $4 level but a "buy" at $33. Today Acclaim is at $21.

Investing in a Quality Stock in a Depressed Industry

In a variation on the same theme, you can make money in depressed industries. Of course, the smart investor won't invest in just any stock. He or she analyzes companies involved in that industry, searching for one that has good growth potential. That way the investor has the opportunity to make a profit as the quality company responds to the normal upward fluctuation when the industry makes a comeback.

For example, the gold industry has always experienced up and down fluctuations. If gold is at a very low price, it should be only a matter of time before that price begins to rise. Locating a quality gold-mining company and purchasing its stock can be very lucrative. In 1979 gold was at $850 per ounce, and people were standing in line at their banks to take money out of their savings to invest in it. By February 1985 gold had fallen to $280 per ounce, and everyone became afraid to invest in gold. After the 1987 crash, gold rose to the $500 level and has cycled down to a recent low of $330 in December 1992.

While I don't pretend to be a gold expert, I realized that $330 was an exceptionally low price for gold and that at some point the cycle would begin an upward trend. Gold stocks were trading at or near their 52-week low prices, and we just had elected a president who won on a platform that claimed we were experiencing the worst economy in 50 years.

The time was ripe to recommend a high-quality gold stock—FMC Gold, which was listed on the NYSE. At $4.13, FMC was a low-priced, conservative stock with excellent fundamentals, including $154 million in cash and securities. Less than three months after my recommendation, the stock had jumped to $7.63 or +85 percent.

In March and April of 1993, gold moved up to the $380 level, and analysts were sounding pretty gloomy about our economic health. Hoards of scared investors began looking for more "solid" investments such as gold. In response, almost all gold stocks soared to their 52-week high.

I cautioned in my newsletter that smart investors were not buying gold stocks at those high prices. They had already bought quality gold stocks after Clinton was elected, when those stocks were near their lows, and were now taking their profits. Since then many gold stocks have tumbled. Investors who followed Wall Street's lead and bought their gold stocks at the 52-week high have seen their investment fall 35 percent or more.

I firmly believe that the investor will do far better buying a quality, low-priced gold stock than investing in gold bullion as a commodity. Investors who bought gold at its low of $330 in 1992 would have made a potential 25 percent profit when it hit its high of approximately $415, while those who bought FMC Gold had an 85 percent increase in a much shorter period of time.

The Contrarian Approach

Individuals who invest in turnaround stocks or depressed industries are known as *contrarians*. As the name implies, this investment philosophy calls for investing contrary to what most investors and Wall Street are doing. The contrarian opinion is that if everyone is certain that something will happen, it won't. This is the art of thinking for yourself, not succumbing to the influence of the crowd. This thinking works in just about any market because human nature is the same everywhere.

In the marketplace, most investors wait until they see mass buying before purchasing the stock themselves. Likewise, they wait until they see mass selling before they get out. (And they wonder why they can't make money in the stock market!) J. Paul Getty expressed this logic in his book, *How To Be Rich*, when he wrote that an investor should "buy when everyone else is selling and hold until everyone else is buying. This is more than a catchy slogan. It is the very essence of successful investment and accumulating wealth."

IDENTIFYING AND SELECTING A QUALITY TURNAROUND

How do you discover the few turnaround stocks that have the potential for good profits? It takes research.

Locating Turnaround Stocks

The easiest way to find possible turnaround companies is to check *The Wall Street Journal, Investor's Business Daily* or *Barron's.* Look through the stock listings for a large spread between the 52-week high and low prices. Locating a stock with a high of $53 and a low of $2.75 indicates that something drastic has happened to the company. It will take further research to determine what it was and if the company has possibilities.

Another way to locate turnaround candidates is to follow the biggest percentage losers for the NYSE. (At least in the beginning I advise that you restrict yourself to NYSE-listed stocks since they are the largest, most profitable and well-known companies.) I like to follow the percentage-losers' column because some of the best turnarounds started out being listed in this column as their prices plunged. You can also review the weekly, monthly and year-end percentage losers that are listed in *Barron's.* Some very well-known companies have been listed in the percentage-losers' column. Another area you may want to check is the earnings reports that are listed on a daily basis in *The Wall Street Journal.* Look for companies that have produced a profit after suffering previous losses. Over a period of time you can accumulate a list of stocks that may be turnarounds, and you'll become familiar with their names and how their stocks trade. The next step involves research to weed out the bad stocks and find those select few that contain the elements for a tremendous stock-price move.

What To Look For in a Turnaround Stock

In August 1982 I researched Grolier, Inc., which was trading on the Philadelphia Exchange at $1.81 per share. Grolier was the world's largest publisher and distributor of quality encyclopedia and reference sets and a leading publisher of children's books and educational items. The company had previously been listed on the NYSE and traded as high as $30. However, Grolier suffered huge losses and moved down from the NYSE to start trading on the Philadelphia Exchange.

Grolier attacked its problems and turned itself around. When I decided it was a great investment, the company had annual sales of $345 million with a net income of $1.31 per share, yet it was selling for only $1.81. Grolier had well-known products and improved sales and earnings; however, Wall Street had failed to realize what a gem the company was at that price. A little later, Grolier applied for relisting on the NYSE, and the stock started to soar. Eventually the company was bought out at $27.50 per share, giving investors a tremendous profit of 1,419 percent.

Another turnaround company was BancTexas Group, a major commercial bank in Dallas and Houston. Listed on the NYSE, in 1987 BancTexas was a high flyer, selling at $62 per share. Then the savings and loan scandal exploded, and BancTexas's stock plunged. I recommended the stock in 1989 at $.31 (yes, it was still listed on the NYSE) at the height of the media hoopla. At that point, the stock was extremely undervalued. It was also showing signs of a turnaround with improvements in its sales and earnings figures. It took three years, but the stock eventually rose to $3.75, for a great 1,200 percent increase.

Most investors, including many brokers, choose turnaround stocks strictly by price. While this is a factor, it is not the only one. I like companies that have established, well-known products, sales of over $100 million and a stock price at perhaps 10 percent of its previous high price.

The most important element is the company's balance sheet. When a stock's price has plunged, it's typically due to unexpected, severe losses. These create negative cash flow, high inventory and large write-offs. It can take a year or several years for the company to correct the problems that caused the losses and turn around its balance sheet. I like to buy a stock that has increased its cash flow and cash position, lowered its inventories and shown a profitable quarter.

I prefer to wait for the release of the positive figures rather than buying earlier when the company's management projects that it will produce a profitable quarter. This tactic was developed from experience when many projected profitable quarters never materialized. In addition, the profits must be from continuing operations, not from tax credits or extraordinary credits. If the company is profitable only because of a big tax credit or an extraordinary credit from selling a division, it really hasn't experienced the turnaround. Its continuing operations will be the final factor in determining whether or not the company maintains its profitability.

Claire's Stores on the NYSE was another turnaround stock recommendation. Through its stores, called Claire's Boutique, it caters to women's fashion accessory needs at very inexpensive prices. The boutiques are located in shopping malls across the country. Claire's Stores was trading for more than $15 per share until it experienced difficulties and declared huge losses. Wall Street reacted by bailing out and causing the stock price to plummet. In February 1988 I recommended Claire's Stores at $3.75, for I saw a good financial turnaround with nine-month sales of $70 million versus $55 million a year ago and net income of $3.6 million or $.18 per share, compared to $1.1 million or $.06 per share the previous year. The stock continued to move upward and hit a 1990 high of $23.88 or +537 percent.

TURNAROUNDS TO AVOID

Not all turnaround stocks are good investments. It is important to know which situations to avoid so you don't lose your money. Probably only about 5 percent of turnaround stocks are excellent candidates with good profit potential. Now there will always be exceptions to the rule, but on the whole, if a company has any of the following going against it, its chances of being a successful turnaround stock are severely limited.

Companies in Industries That Are Very Capital Intensive

It is hard enough for a company to turn around its sales and earnings, create assets and working capital and lower its debt; but when the company is in an industry that requires a lot of capital, this can be too much to handle. For example, if the company is in the entertainment, high-technology, real estate or pharmaceutical industry, where a large amount of working capital may be needed, and it can't obtain the capital through sales, it may be forced to issue more shares of securities or go further into debt. Either way, the shareholder value is negatively affected by dilution.

I discovered a good example of this when I recommended Wessex Corporation in August 1987 at $2.50. The company owns and manages many health-care facilities in the southeastern part of the United States. When I recommended Wessex, it had just returned to profitability with a good increase in sales and earnings. The stock price did move up to $4.50 after the recommendation. However, Wessex posted a loss the following quarter and continued to raise necessary capital by going further and further into debt. That eventually caused the stock to fall. The last time I saw Wessex's stock, it was selling for pennies.

The entertainment industry takes a great deal of capital to produce films. DeLaurentis Films was at one time a major name in the motion-picture industry. Its stock sold for more than $35, but because it needed an extremely high amount of capital to continue producing films, DeLaurentis' debt soared and finally caused the company to enter bankruptcy.

Companies in the real estate and high-technology industries also need huge amounts of working capital. In most cases their stock prices are several times the companies' book value. In particular, the book value for real estate companies can be greatly exaggerated and unrealistic. Pharmaceutical companies invest huge sums on research and development and then still have to spend years testing their drugs before they obtain Food and Drug Administration (FDA) approval to sell the drugs to the public. Often a company will run out of money before it obtains FDA approval to market the drug to the public and generate income.

Companies That Have an Extremely Large Debt

Many times the stocks that plunge are ones with debts large enough that they can't make the payments anymore. Not only does the company have to turn around its sales and earnings; it has to placate its creditors.

Since the only real asset the company may have when it restructures debt is its common shares, management may decide to issue additional shares to its creditors. This dilutes the shareholder value.

Even worse, management could decide to totally restructure the company by issuing new shares. If this happens, the old common shares become worthless. Companies such as Continental Airlines, Ames Department Stores, Wang Labs and Emerson Radio have all resorted to this strategy to decrease debt. It's amazing that they can wipe out their current common shareholders, issue new shares in a restructured company and continue to do business. It certainly doesn't seem fair to the common shareholders who suddenly find that their investment has no value.

Companies That Offer High Dividends

This is a trap that catches many unsuspecting blue chip investors. They get caught when they look through the newspaper for low-priced stocks paying high-percentage dividends. They don't realize that most of the time the dividend percentage is inflated because the stock has suffered losses and its price has plunged. The dividend percentage (which is based on the previous dividend when the company was making more money) moves up in response to the lower price, giving a very false impression. Many times, the investors find a high-percentage dividend and don't research the stock to see whether it has the cash to pay the dividend. If the company's price has just fallen to a much lower level, the reason usually is huge losses and debt. Needless to say, those losses may prevent the company from paying any further dividends for a while. When the company suspends or discontinues its dividend, the stock price can plunge even further, and the investor has lost all around.

Companies Affected by Foreign Currency

Two types of companies fall into this category. The first is a company that purchases all its products from foreign countries. Over the past few years, with the rapid fluctuation of the U.S. dollar, companies experienced huge losses just because the U.S. dollar's value declined.

The second type of company to bypass is one that sells the majority of its products to foreign countries and is paid in foreign currency. The fluctuation in the value of the U.S. dollar can severely impact the company's revenues and threaten its profits.

Companies That Are Recommended as Hot Tips

Always be careful of tips from any source. Don't take anyone else's word that a turnaround (or for that matter, any stock) is a great investment without doing your own research. If you are going to invest your hard-earned cash, it is worth the effort to ask the person with the hot tip to send financial and general information (the annual report, 10-K and 10-Q reports and latest press releases) on the company for you to analyze.

Turnaround stocks can give the knowledgeable investor enormous profits if he or she takes the time to carefully research and analyze the stock. If he or she doesn't, the investor is destined to lose money in the long run.

CHAPTER

10

Mastering Warrants

In September 1986 I recommended both the common stock and the warrant of Medco Research. At that time the common stock was selling at $2.50 per share and the warrant was $.75. Over the next six months Medco's common stock moved up to $25.25 or +910 percent! That's very impressive. However, Medco's warrant moved from $.75 to $22 or +2,833 percent.

Example: If you had $1,000 to invest, you could have bought 400 shares of Medco's common stock and would have had a potential value of $10,100. At $.75, you could have bought 1,333 warrants, which would have skyrocketed up to a $29,326 value. That's over three times the profit.

In general, warrants sell at a very low price in comparison to the common stock. Good price moves in the common stock often can result in tremendous price and percentage moves in the warrant.

In September 1993 Centocor Inc. was selling at $7 per share, and its warrant was at $2. Over the next three months Centocor's stock moved from $7 to $15 or +115 percent. Meanwhile, its warrant skyrocketed from $2 to $15 or +750 percent!

Example: If you had $3,500 to invest, you could have bought 500 shares of Centocor's common stock and would have had a potential value of $7,500. At $2, you could have bought 1,750 warrants, which would have jumped up to a $26,250 value. That's over three times the profit!

DEFINITION OF A WARRANT AND ITS VALUE

Many companies offering new issues will do so in units, which is the combination of one or more common shares plus one or more warrants. What is a *warrant*? It is the right (but not the obligation) to buy usually one share of common stock at a specific price until a specific expiration date. Warrants can be bought and sold in the same way as stocks. They do not participate in profits, do not pay dividends and offer no voting privileges. The warrant's value, if any, is derived from the upward price movement of the common stock.

CRITERIA FOR ANALYZING AND SELECTING WARRANTS

Before purchasing a warrant, it is important to make sure the company you are investing in is a high-quality and low-priced company. If the stock price is already near its 52-week high, your profit potential will be greatly reduced. Once you have determined that the company is a good investment and the price is right, you can begin to analyze its warrants. When analyzing warrants, you must be concerned with three components:

1. *Exercise price.* This is the price at which the warrant is exercised to buy one share of common stock. In other words, this is the price you have to pay to get one share of common stock.
2. *Expiration date.* This is the date by which you must exercise the warrant. The longer the time period before the expiration date, the greater the opportunity for the stock price to move upward, making the warrant more valuable.
3. *Volatility.* The more volatile the common stock is, the greater the chance the stock price will jump up, increasing the value of the warrant.

These three components can make the difference between a profit and a loss. If you buy a warrant with an exercise price of $3 per share and an expiration date of September 30, 1998, you are betting that the common stock will move significantly above its current price before September 30, 1998. The closer the exercise price is to the current stock price and the longer the time period before the warrant expires, the greater your potential for good profits. Of course, if the stock is volatile, the possibility for profits increases.

Perhaps the most important factor in purchasing a warrant is to choose a good-quality company whose stock is currently undervalued. The warrant price is totally dependent on the price of the common stock, so it is vital that the common stock price is low and has a good potential to move upward. No matter how low the warrant price, don't buy it unless you also consider the common stock to be a good investment.

FACTORS THAT MAKE WARRANTS MOVE UP OR DOWN

When a warrant is about to expire, a company may try to raise its common stock price up above the warrant's exercise price. If investors can purchase the common stock through the warrant for less than it would cost on the market, they will exercise the warrant, and that delivers capital for the company's use. It is not uncommon for the stock price to plunge after the warrant expires because the upward price movement was artificially created by the company.

> **Example:**   One bargain-priced stock jumped from $.09 to $.63 over a six-month period. The company decided to exercise its warrant at $.50. In other words, investors could buy a share of common stock for $.50 rather than the then-current $.63 selling price. The smart people took advantage of the opportunity and sold their warrants at huge profits. The not-so-smart people exercised their warrants at $.50 per share only to see the stock fall from $.63 to $.20 in a matter of weeks.

Therefore, *the real money is made in selling a warrant—not in exercising it.* If a company wants to exercise a warrant that you own, say "thanks, but no thanks," and take your profit by selling your warrant.

HOW TO FIND WARRANTS

The easiest way to locate warrants is to look through the stocks listed on the NYSE, AMEX or Nasdaq in the financial section of any major

Figure 10.1   Centocor Listing

52-Week		Company	Closing
High	Low	Name	Price
19½	5¼	Centocor Inc.	11⅞
19¾	1⁵⁄₁₆	Centocor Inc. Wt	8½

newspaper, *The Wall Street Journal, Investors' Business Daily* or *Barron's.*
The newspapers list warrants under the company's common stock and
indicate the warrants by a *Wt* after the name. Figure 10.1 shows the
common stock of Centocor Inc. and its warrant, designated by a *Wt*
after the name.

Sometimes a company has more than one warrant. Then the
warrant will be designated by a *Wt* with an *A, B,* etc., or the year of
expiration after it. Figure 10.2 shows Industrial Holdings common
stock and two warrants.

In most cases a company's warrant will be listed immediately
below the common stock. Occasionally the warrant will be listed on
another exchange, as shown in Figure 10.3.

Warrants usually are included in a new-issue offering as part of a
unit. When the unit starts trading, it can be broken into its components. If the unit was composed of two shares of common stock and
one warrant, it may look like Figure 10.4.

When the warrant is either called in or exercised by the company,
it, of course no longer trades. However, it will be listed for a while in
the papers, as shown in Figure 10.5. Some NYSE warrants that are
currently listed in the financial pages of *The Wall Street Journal* are in
Figure 10.6.

As you can see, the warrant price is extremely small compared to
the stock price. When you have a certain amount of money that you

Figure 10.2   Industrial Holdings Listing

52-Week		Company	Closing
High	Low	Name	Price
4¾	3⅛	Industrial Holdings	4⅛
1⁵⁄₁₆	½	Industrial Holdings Wt A	11⁄₁₆
7⁄₁₆	3⁄₁₆	Industrial Holdings Wt B	13⁄₃₂

Figure 10.3   Listings on Different Exchanges

52-Week High	Low	Company Name	Closing Price	Exchange
10½	6	Amax Gold	6⅞	NYSE
1⅞	½	Amax Gold Wt	1¹⁄₁₆	AMEX
5¼	2½	Atlas Corp	4¼	NYSE
2¼	⅝	Atlas Corp Wt	1¼	AMEX

want to invest, purchasing a warrant on a good undervalued stock can give you more buying power.

WARRANTS VERSUS OPTIONS

Many people have a hard time understanding the difference between warrants and options. They are similar, but with a couple of important differences.

A warrant is the right (but not the obligation) to buy usually one share of a specific stock for a specific price until a specific expiration date. The expiration date can be several years in the future.

An *option* is the right (but not the obligation) to buy 100 shares of a specific stock for a specific price until a specific expiration date. A typical option will have an expiration date from three to nine months in the future.

The important element is the time limit. Because most investors who buy options or warrants are doing so to trade rather than to exercise them, once the warrants expire, they have no trading value. Therefore, it makes sense that the more time you have to trade the

Figure 10.4   Unit Listing

52-Week High	Low	Company Name	Closing Price
5⅓	3	Grace Health	3
1⅝	⁹⁄₁₆	Grace Health Wt	¹¹⁄₁₆
12¼	6⅝	Grace Health Un	6⅝

Figure 10.5   Listing of Exercised Warrant

52-Week		Company	Closing
High	Low	Name	Price
5¼	1¾	ABC Company	4½
½	¼	ABC Company Wt	. . .

security, the better your chance of making a profit. I suggest purchasing warrants that have at least two years remaining until the expiration date. An additional advantage of warrants is that the commission rate is usually much less than that charged for options. The warrant is a more conservative investment than the option. Warrants generally have the potential for superior gains for a small amount of money. If you have found a quality, low-priced stock that you are considering as an investment, always check to see if it has any warrants.

Figure 10.6   Sample NYSE Warrants

52-Week		Company	Closing
High	Low	Name	Price
10⅜	6⅞	ADT	8⅞
2	¾	ADT Wt	¹³⁄₁₆
17½	7¼	CarterHaw	9½
5¾	2⅜	CarterHaw Wt	3⅞
19¾	14⅝	EnquirStar	19
2⅝	1½	EnquirStar Wt	2
21⅛	16⅞	Hanson	20
3⅛	1⅛	Hanson Wt	2⅜
16¼	10	LTV Cp	16⅛
4¼	3	LTV Cp Wt	4⅛
18⅝	8¾	MagmaCopper	13¼
11⅝	3⅞	MagmaCopper Wt	7⅝
22¾	10⅞	Safeway	21¼
5¼	2	Safeway Wt	4⅞
30½	9⅝	USG	29¼
17⅜	3	USG Wt	16¾
29	19	US Home	26⅝
16	6½	US Home Wt B	13⅜

CHAPTER

11

Choosing the Best Broker for Your Needs

Brokerage firms have come a long way from the days when they strictly bought and sold stocks for their customers. Today most types of personal financial services are available through one kind of brokerage firm or another, including life insurance, real estate partnerships, mutual funds, financial planning and even checking accounts. Selecting the best broker for your needs takes a little planning and effort, but it could be one of the most important decisions you make.

You must first decide what kind of investor you are and would like to be and where you plan to go with your trading. Are you a novice? Do you want investment advice from your broker, or would you prefer to pick your own investments? The answers to these questions will determine whether you need a broker who charges higher commissions but offers investment advice or just the least-expensive broker available to execute your investment trade.

FULL-SERVICE VERSUS DISCOUNT BROKERS

There are distinct differences between full-service and discount brokers. The *full-service broker* offers personal service. He or she will recommend specific stocks or investment strategies tailored to your financial needs and the size of your account. A full-service broker normally has more services available to help inexperienced investors.

In general, full-service brokers charge up to 10 percent of the price of the trade with a $50 minimum commission. Certain full-service brokers may slightly reduce their normal commission fees to their larger clients. (A full-service broker usually receives no salary but instead receives about 30 percent of the total commission fee.) Many full-service brokerage firms have recently tried to bring in more income by charging clients a monthly account fee, mailing fees and even trade-confirmation fees.

A *discount broker* buys and sells stock for you at a lower commission rate, typically 25 to 80 percent less than the full-service fee with a $40 to $50 minimum commission. (The larger the amount of the trade, the greater the discount.) He or she generally does not recommend specific securities or strategies and offers no individual investment counseling or financial planning. The discount broker won't care about your personal balance sheet, and since he or she receives a salary instead of part of the commission fee, the discount broker won't solicit your business to increase his or her paycheck.

Over the past few years the discount brokerage industry has added services and increased commission fees. Firms such as Charles Schwab offer many extra services, but these are near the higher end of the discount commission scale, charging 5 or 6 percent. This is still cheaper than the 10 percent charged by full-service brokerage firms. Many discount brokers have significantly raised their fees for trading lower-priced stocks.

This increase has created a niche for a new type of brokerage firm called a *deep-discount broker,* which charges from $.015 to $.03 per share. Many of these firms offer the ability to punch in your buy or sell order over your home computer or Touch-Tone telephone. Deep-discount brokers offer the least amount of services but the best prices. For example, I recently bought 5,000 shares of a $1 stock from a major discount brokerage firm and paid a commission of $270. However, buying the same 5,000 shares from a deep-discount brokerage firm cost only $75. This really adds up when you consider the savings for both buying and selling the stock.

With the passage of time, certain discount brokerage firms have begun to offer more and more services. Typically, the more services that are offered, the higher the commissions charged to cover the costs of the additional services. As an investor, you don't want to pay higher commissions for services you won't be using. However, if you are inexperienced, it may be well worth the additional cost to get a broker who will help you make wise investment decisions.

FINDING, KEEPING AND WORKING WITH A BROKER

Just as you would search for high quality and value in a new car or home, you also should shop around for a good broker. After all, you are going to trust the broker with your money, so you want to be sure that he or she is honest and will give you profitable advice and service. If you are very knowledgeable about the stock market and know exactly what you want to buy and sell, then you basically want an "order taker" who will execute your trades, and your main consideration will be commission. However, if you need more help in making wise investment decisions, you need more than an order taker. The following information will guide you in finding the right broker for your needs.

Locating the Right Broker for You

First you must decide what type of broker you need. Do you need advice on your investments? If so, a full-service broker should be your choice. If you know what you want to buy, a discount or even deep-discount broker may be best for you.

Your next step is to find some good candidates from which to choose your personal broker. You can ask for referrals from friends who invest, your tax accountant or professional acquaintances who are involved in the market, such as your banker. If you don't know anyone who can recommend a broker, you can refer to the list of brokerage firms (in Figures 11.1, 11.2 and 11.3) that have excellent reputations for employing honest brokers. If you live in a larger city, many of these firms will have a branch office that you can locate by looking in your local telephone directory. If not, use the telephone number to call the brokerage firm at its main office. (Some brokerage firms frequently change their telephone numbers. If you try a number and it is no longer correct, call directory assistance to request the current telephone number.)

A Full-Service Broker   If you are calling a full-service broker who was recommended, you should say to him or her, "John Smith gave me your name." You'll want to inquire about which types of investments he or she specializes in, indicate how much you want to invest and request that the broker send you several ideas.

As a courteous client, you should call to interview your broker candidate after the market is closed. That way you won't be depriving

Figure 11.1 Full-Service Brokerage Firms

Bear Stearns & Co. 245 Park Avenue New York, NY 10167 212-272-2000	Kemper Securities 77 West Wacker Drive Chicago, IL 60601 312-574-6000	PaineWebber 1285 Avenue of the Americas New York, NY 10019 212-713-2000
William Blair & Co. 222 W. Adams St. Chicago, IL 60606 312-236-1600	Kidder, Peabody & Co. Incorporated 10 Hanover Square New York, NY 10005 212-510-3000	Prudential Securities, Inc. One Seaport Plaza 199 Water Street New York, NY 10292 212-214-1000
Dean Witter Reynolds Inc. 2 World Trade Center New York, NY 10048 212-392-2222	Merrill Lynch Inc. World Trade Center, North Tower New York, NY 10281 212-449-1000	Smith Barney Shearson Inc. 1345 Avenue of the Americas New York, NY 10105 212-399-6000
A. G. Edwards & Sons, Inc. One North Jefferson Street St. Louis, MO 63103 314-289-3000	Oppenheimer & Company, Inc. Oppenheimer Tower One World Financial Center New York, NY 10281 212-667-7000	Lehman Brothers, Inc. American Express Tower C World Financial Center 200 Vesey St. New York, NY 10285 212-298-2000

him or her of the opportunity to make a commission from another client who wants to buy or sell stock.

If you are calling a full-service brokerage firm, you should realize that most firms have a "broker of the day," who takes calls from individuals who haven't asked for a specific broker. You'll need to ask that broker which investment areas he or she specializes in and discuss how much you have to invest. You can request that he or she send you some investment ideas for consideration.

Be careful of any broker who pushes you to buy immediately. (You want service, not pressure, from a broker.) Also avoid any broker who insists that you invest a minimum of $5,000 to $10,000 with him or her. (You want a broker who is willing to help you even if you only have only $1,000 to invest.)

Once you have at least three broker candidates, interview each candidate and discuss in depth his or her strategy for handling your account. The broker needs to know how much you expect to have available for investments and what type of investments you want to make, so make these decisions before talking to the broker. If you are a small investor, don't be embarrassed. In 1990 a NYSE survey found that over 40 percent of all investors invest less than $10,000.

Figure 11.2 Discount Brokerage Firms

Brown & Company
20 Winthrop Square
  2nd Floor
Boston, MA 02110
617-742-2600

Burke Christensen & Lewis
  Securities
303 W. Madison, 4th Floor
Chicago, IL 60606
312-346-8283

Charles Schwab & Co. Inc.
101 Montgomery Street
San Francisco, CA 94104
415-627-7000

Fidelity Investments
82 Devonshire Street
Boston, MA 02109
617-570-7000

Kennedy Cabot & Company
9470 Wilshire Boulevard
Beverly Hills, CA 90212
310-550-0711

Muriel Siebert & Co.
885 Third Ave., Suite 1720
New York, NY 10022
800-USA-0711

Olde Discount Stockbrokers
751 Griswold St.
Detroit, MI 48226
313-961-6666

Pacific Brokerage Services
5757 Wilshire Boulevard,
  Suite 3
Los Angeles, CA 90036
800-421-8395

Quick & Reilly, Inc.
230 S. County Road
Palm Beach, FL 33480
407-655-8000

StockCross
One Washington Mall
Boston, MA 02108
617-367-5700

Waterhouse Securities, Inc.
100 Wall Street
New York, NY 10005
212-806-3500

Don't be intimidated by an impressive office or a smooth sales pitch. Discuss your financial goals and investment capabilities completely with the broker. He or she should express interest in your financial status and your personal taste in investment strategies. To help you get started, here is a list of some questions that you can ask your broker candidate:

- How long have you been in the securities industry? How long have you been with this brokerage firm? Where did you work before?
- Where do you get investment recommendations? Do you research them yourself or rely on others?
- Do you have any client references?
- How many clients do you have? Are you readily accessible by telephone to handle my transactions?
- What specifics do you look for before giving a buy or sell recommendation? What's your philosophy for profit taking?
- How are the firm's commission fees figured? Are there any discounts? Are there any other charges for services or monthly fees?
- What services are offered by your brokerage firm? Does it have in-house personnel to research and analyze companies and market trends?

Figure 11.3   Deep-Discount Brokerage Firms

AccuTrade
4211 South 102nd Street
Omaha, NE 68127-1031
402-331-2526

R. J. Forbes Group
150 Broad Hollow Road
Melville, NY 11747
800-488-0090

Pacific Brokerage Services
   Inc.
5757 Wilshire Boulevard,
   Suite 3
Los Angeles, CA 90036
800-262-2294

E*Trade Securities
480 California Avenue,
   3rd Floor
Palo Alto, CA 94306
415-326-2700
800-786-2575

Lombard Institutional
   Brokerage
One Second Street
San Francisco, CA
94105-3407
800-688-6896

Regal Discount Securities,
   Inc.
209 W. Jackson Street,
   Suite 906
Chicago, IL 60606
312-554-2240
800-786-9000

- What's the financial condition of the brokerage firm? (Ask for the latest annual and quarterly reports.) Is it a member of any recognized national stock exchange? Does it belong to the NASD and the Securities Investors Protection Corporation (SIPC)?
- What do the monthly customer statements include?

You're the only one who can judge whether the broker's services, investment guidance and commission fees are compatible with your own investment objectives. If you want to invest in stocks under $10 per share, make sure your broker is satisfied with buying low-priced stocks. Your goal is to find a broker who is honest, efficient, dependable and, most importantly, feels responsible about the capital you are investing.

A Discount Broker   If you are an individual who makes your own investment decisions, you want to find a discount brokerage firm. Because the brokers at discount firms basically are order takers, you'll be more interested in the commission schedule. Contact several firms to ask for information about opening an account. They should send detailed literature explaining their services and commission fees. Comparing the information from each discount brokerage firm should give you the basis to make an intelligent decision as to which to use.

There's no law against having more than one broker. In fact, if you have only one broker, it's hard to gauge how well he or she is doing. Many investors employ two or more brokers whom they use for different investments. You may also want to consider using a discount broker to execute your trades when you know exactly what you want to buy and contacting a full-service broker for help in choosing other investments. (I believe that it is very inconsiderate for an investor to buy a full-service broker's investment recommendation from a discount brokerage firm to save commission fees. If your broker made the recommendation, you should buy the stock from him or her.)

Beware of the Unethical Broker

As recent scandals on Wall Street have revealed, brokers (and some brokerage firms) are just as susceptible to dishonesty and prone to mismanagement as are any other professionals who routinely handle large sums of money. In headline after headline we read about brokers who didn't resist the temptation to excessively trade a client's stocks for the additional commission fees. In some instances brokers have "borrowed" from customers' accounts to invest in a hot tip or swindled clients by convincing them to invest in worthless stocks.

> **Example:**   A housewife wanted to recover a $900 loss on an investment. She gave her broker (who worked for a major firm) permission (she claimed it was unwitting permission) to trade extremely speculative uncovered stock index options on her behalf. Her risk became apparent on October 19, 1987 (Black Monday), when her broker called and told her that she now owed almost $170,000 on her options account that he had handled! An equitable settlement was finally worked out; however, most investors are not so lucky.

When you have found a broker with whom you feel comfortable, you should check with your local branch of the NASD to make sure that no complaints or sanctions have been brought against him or her. (The NASD has an office located in each state, usually in the capital or major city. You can obtain its telephone number from directory assistance.)

It is easy for an unethical broker to take advantage of the inexperienced investor. The broker can charge the highest possible commission rates and say they are the best available. If the investor doesn't check that statement, he or she will never know if it's true or not. After you get your broker's fees for a particular trade, you can call a few other brokers to ask for their rates on the same trade. This can help you determine whether your broker is giving you a good commission rate. Of course, if he or she is giving you special advice, even if the fees are higher, the broker may be well worth the additional cost.

Opening an Account

Before you make any transactions with your new broker, you will probably need to complete a new account form, which is required by the SEC. Figure 11.4 shows the questions most likely to be asked. While some of the questions may seem awfully nosy, they're for your protection. Your broker must know your financial situation to decide which types of investments would best fit your circumstances.

Just because you have confidence in your broker, you shouldn't ignore your investments. After all, mistakes can happen, especially in the hectic day-to-day rat race of a brokerage house. However, if the same mistake (or mistakes in general) keep occurring, you've found a bad broker and should terminate your relationship. Remember, the brokerage community is a free market, and you are at liberty to move from one broker to another as you please.

If you feel uncomfortable with your brokerage house or broker or feel you are pressured by them, don't feel guilty about taking your account elsewhere. Your financial future is at stake, and that comes first. Never stay with a broker if your relationship ceases to be potentially profitable.

Taking Possession of Your Stock Certificates

While your broker will keep your stock certificates for you, I recommend that you request that the stock certificates be put in your name and sent to you. Granted, you will have to rent a safe-deposit box (if you don't already have one) to hold the certificates, but this request carries three advantages:

1. You can evaluate your broker's efficiency by how promptly you receive the certificates. (Three to six weeks is normal.)
2. Having the certificates put in your name should ensure that you receive the annual and quarterly reports along with press releases. If your certificate is kept in the street name, your broker is supposed to forward that information to you when he or she

Figure 11.4   A Typical New Customer Account Application

Date: _____   Branch Office Location : _____

Type of Account:
_____ Individual   _____ Partnership
_____ Joint   _____ Uniform Gift to Minors
_____ Corporation   _____ Trust

Name: _____
                    Last   First   Middle Initial

Spouse: _____
                    Last   First   Middle Initial

Mailing Address: _____

_____

  City _____   State _____   Zip ____
Home Address (if different): _____

_____

  City _____   State _____   Zip ____

Employer:_____

  Address _____

  City _____   State _____   Zip ____

  Position _____

Telephone:
Work _____   Home _____

Bank Reference: _____   Account # _____
Estimated Total Annual Income: _____   Joint _____
Estimated Net Worth: _____   Joint _____
Number of Years Investing: _____
Investment Objectives:
_____ Speculative   _____ Mutual Funds
_____ Income   _____ Trading
_____ Stocks   _____ Bonds

Signature: _____
            Social Security Number _____

receives it from the company. Some brokers are very religious about sending these materials to shareholders; many aren't.

3. Perhaps the main reason to ask for your stock certificates is to avoid delays if the brokerage firm that is holding them goes under. Over the past few years many brokerage firms (even some with fine reputations) have found themselves in financial trouble and have closed their doors. Investors are protected by the SIPC, and they will eventually receive all monies and stock certificates that the brokerage firm was holding for them. However, it takes time to sort through all the company's books and forward the certificates and proceeds. The procedure can take from three to nine months. During that time the investor cannot sell his or her stock because he or she does not have the certificate.

Sometimes a broker may resist your request to have the stock certificate sent to you because the broker believes that if she retains the certificate, you will sell the stock through her, and she will get the commission. (If the broker has given you good advice and service, she deserves the commission.) However, holding the certificate yourself gives you the option to sell the stock at any time through any broker.

Locating a good broker can be a time-consuming process, but the wise investor will make the effort to find an honest, knowledgeable broker with whom he or she feels comfortable. Because the average investor does not fully understand the risks involved in investments such as options, commodities, futures and penny stocks, his or her broker is obligated both ethically and legally to know the client and suggest investments suitable for the client's situation.

Your broker must be readily available for your calls. If he or she doesn't have time to take your orders during a regular day, imagine the type of service you would get during a crisis like the 1987 crash. Remember, a broker will give his or her best clients the best service. If you are a small investor, you need a broker who will work hard to service your account, even if it is modest.

CHAPTER

12

How and When To Buy Stocks

Buying the right stock for the right price is the key to making a good profit. Unfortunately, most individuals spend too much time trying to determine where the market is going and not enough time analyzing whether the current stock price is a good value. After investigating several stocks and determining that they are quality companies, the smart investor doesn't just enter a buy order at the market price. He or she takes the time to establish a target price near the 52-week low and waits for the stock to reach it.

HOW TO BUY STOCKS

After choosing the stock you want to buy, it is important to completely understand the process involved in purchasing stocks.

The Size of Your Stock Order

You must determine how many shares of stock you want to purchase. The amount of money you have to invest and the price of the stock will limit the number of shares you can buy. Depending on the size of your investment capital, you should consider diversifying by purchasing three or more stocks. (If you are starting out with only $1,000 to invest, you will want to use it all for one stock. If you have $10,000, you can easily diversify into two, three or four stocks.) I advise that you begin with smaller amounts until you are confident that you are investing wisely.

Always buy stock in a round lot, which is the standard trading unit for stocks and warrants. Round lots are sold by hundreds. Therefore, you can purchase stocks in any multiple of 100, such as 100, 200, 300, 1,000, 1,200, etc. If you buy 1 to 99 shares, this is considered an odd lot, and usually you will pay a higher commission. In most cases an investor buying an odd lot (say 75 shares) will end up paying an extra eighth of a point when both buying and selling the stock. If you want to purchase 275 shares, this would be bought in a round lot of 200 shares and an odd lot of 75 shares. Because of the increased commission fees, I recommend buying only in round lots.

Another consideration in buying stock is that if you buy only a few shares, the commission fee can consume a good portion of your profit. The commission scale typically favors buying more shares, and in most cases, the commission to purchase 1,000 shares of stock may be only two or three times as much as the commission to purchase 100 shares. Therefore, I suggest purchasing 1,000 shares or more if possible.

Type of Buy Order

Once you have determined what stock you want to buy and approximately how many shares you want, you must decide what price you want to pay. You can enter your order a couple of different ways.

Market Order

The vast majority of all stock orders are executed by *market orders*. Very simply, you call your broker and authorize him or her to enter your order to buy at the best price available at the time your order reaches the floor of the stock exchange (in other words, at the market price). Market orders usually are given top priority on the communication systems of most brokers and can usually be executed in just a few minutes. This occurs so quickly that the broker may ask you to hold on the telephone while he or she completes the transaction.

Limit Order

If you prefer to set a specific purchase price for the stock, this is called a *limit order.* For example, you call your broker and learn that the stock price is $1.75, but you wanted to buy it at $1.50. You can enter a limit order specifying the $1.50 price that you are willing to pay for the stock. On the other hand, if you like the $1.75 price but don't want to pay any more than that, you can also enter a limit order specifying $1.75. The limit order can be good for the day, month or until executed or canceled. While the limit order can save you some of the purchase price, there is no guarantee that the stock will drop down to the price you have set, and you may miss buying into it.

HOW TO BUY THE RIGHT STOCK AT THE RIGHT PRICE

The purchase price of a stock determines how much profit you will make. You can select a quality stock, but if it is currently selling near its high price, your chances of making a good profit are very small.

□   **RULE 8**   □

Consider the purchase price of a stock to determine your profit.

Most stocks are *cyclical*—they tend to go up and down in price—and normally only a tremendously positive occurrence would cause the stock to move a good deal higher than its 52-week high. Unless something drastic happens to the company, its stock will typically move up near the 52-week high, gradually fall near the 52-week low and then start back up again. Therefore, it is essential to set a target price near the stock's low and wait for the stock to meet that price before purchasing it. You also want a stock that shows at least a 100 percent spread between its 52-week high and low price; otherwise, the stock price may not move enough to make it a good investment.

How do you determine the target price? Look at the 52-week high and low, and compare it to the current price. For example, a stock is selling at $2 a share, and its 52-week high is $8.75. Its 52-week low is $1.13. You might set a target price at $1.50, which is about 25 percent below the current $2 price and near the 52-week low. If the stock falls to $1.50, you purchase it; then when the stock moves back up to $2, instead of just breaking even, you are already ahead 33 percent.

Of course, there's no guarantee that the stock will go down to $1.50. However, I have found this technique to work about 70 percent of the time. When you are trying to buy a stock near the low point of its cycle, it is possible that the stock will go even lower after you purchase it. By setting a target price below its current price, you are at least partially protecting yourself. Buying your stock at the right price is a critical factor in maximizing your profits.

PATIENCE AND DISCIPLINE PAYS

You've found a great little company that has so much potential; your only problem is that its price is high. Now comes the difficult part. You have to ignore that money burning a hole in your pocket and wait for the stock to fall to your target price. This takes a lot of discipline and patience, but it pays in the long run.

☐   **RULE 9**   ☐

Being patient can pay off in profits.

I will sometimes follow a stock for a year or more before it hits the perfect combination of being a high-quality company with a low price. It takes discipline to wait for the right price, but this can make the difference between profits and losses.

Patience and discipline are certainly major factors in the difference between an average and an exceptional investor. One of the investment classes that I taught was a five-week course specializing in low-priced stocks. During the first class I asked my students not to buy any stocks until they finished the course and had a much greater understanding of that type of investment. By the fourth class I would ask the students if they had followed my advice and resisted investing in all the stocks we had discussed as examples. They didn't have to raise their hands; I could tell by the sheepish grins on their faces. In most cases one-half of the students didn't have the discipline to wait.

Too many investors hear a story about a "great stock" and have neither the patience nor the discipline to check it out. Instead, they rush to buy the stock "before it soars" and are greatly disappointed when the stock turns out to be a flop. How many times has someone told you about an unbelievable stock that is going to make you a lot of money if you invest? I know that I have been tempted by such stories. However, if I actually investigated the stock, it usually was a poor investment risk. Perhaps the main reason why boiler-room brokers are so successful selling penny stocks, commodities, futures, worthless oil and gas stocks and other scams is that they know the average investor has no patience. Rather than exercising a little discipline to analyze the stock, the foolish investor gets so wrapped up thinking about the money he or she can make that the investor loses his or her good sense.

In my business I get several calls each day from brokers or companies' officers telling me how wonderful their stocks are. I have learned to never let a good stock story overwhelm my discipline. I always ask that information be sent to me so I can analyze the stock myself before making any investment decision. This strategy has saved me a lot of trouble and money.

DOLLAR COST AVERAGING

Dollar cost averaging is among the simplest and oldest of all formula plans. It basically consists of investing a constant amount of money in stocks over a long period of time, regardless of the level of the stocks' prices. This technique allows an investor to realize profits as long as market prices fluctuate and the same dollar amount of investments continues to be purchased periodically.

For example, an individual has $4,000 to invest each year and buys $1,000 of a stock each quarter. As the stock price rises, fewer shares can be bought with the $1,000; and when the stock's price dips lower, more shares can be bought.

The example in Figure 12.1 shows a typical variation in a stock's price. For dollar cost averaging to work, two ingredients are necessary. First, the security's price must be volatile, and it should be on an upward trend. Money cannot be made on a stock whose price shows a continuous downward trend. By diversifying your portfolio, you greatly reduce this danger.

Second, the investor must be willing and able to purchase securities of an equal dollar amount when stock prices are low as well as

Figure 12.1   Typical Variation in a Stock's Price

Quarter	Amount Invested	Market Price	Shares Bought	Total Owned	Total Invested	Value
1	$1,000.00	$2.50	400	400	$1,000.00	$ 1,000.00
2	1,000.00	3.00	333	733	2,000.00	2,199.00
3	1,000.00	4.00	250	983	3,000.00	3,932.00
4	1,000.00	3.25	307	1,290	4,000.00	4,192.50
5	1,000.00	3.00	333	1,623	5,000.00	4,869.00
6	1,000.00	3.75	266	1,889	6,000.00	7,083.75
7	1,000.00	4.00	250	2,139	7,000.00	8,556.00
8	1,000.00	4.25	235	2,374	8,000.00	10,089.50

high. In a depression salaries may be cut, and the money available to follow the plan may be reduced or totally lacking at the very time when stock prices are at their lowest and therefore most-attractive level.

The success of dollar cost averaging hinges on being able to liquidate the portfolio when the securities' prices are high. The investor can increase big profit potential by planning to liquidate the portfolio several years before it is needed. Thus, the investor can delay the final liquidation if a stock's price level is too low.

Buying securities through a monthly investment plan is a type of dollar cost averaging. It is also a great type of forced savings plan. The periodic buying of mutual fund shares and regular contributions to a pension fund that invests in common stocks could also be classified as a type of dollar-cost-averaging program.

HOW TO AVERAGE DOWN

A major difficulty in purchasing stocks is that the investor has no way of knowing what low price the stock will hit before it turns around and starts its upward cycle. Unless you own a crystal ball that reveals that information, about all you can do is make an educated guess and hope you are right. However, there is a strategy that can prove useful.

When you purchase a stock, consider buying only half as many shares. Then if the price falls, you can buy more shares at the lower price and bring down your break-even point. Your *break-even point* is the average price paid for all shares of stock. (If you bought 1,000 shares at $1.75, your break-even point would be $1.75.) Once the stock

Figure 12.2   Averaging-Down Example

1,000 shares at $1.75	= $1,750
1,555 shares at $1.13	= $1,750 $3,500 ÷ 2,555 shares = $1.37 average price
2,555 shares	$3,500

price moves above the break-even point, you are making a profit. Of course, before buying any more stock, first determine that nothing dreadful has happened to the company, causing the price to fall. After reanalyzing the company and concluding that it is only a normal price fluctuation, then and only then should you consider averaging down.

For example, if you had $3,500 and wanted to purchase 2,000 shares of Global Marine at $1.75 per share, instead of buying all 2,000 shares at once, you purchase just 1,000 shares at $1.75. This leaves you some available cash to purchase more shares if the stock price falls. This happened after one of my Global Marine recommendations. You could have purchased the first 1,000 shares at $1.75 asked, leaving $1,750 for further investment. Sure enough, the stock fell to $1.13, and if you bought at that price, your $1,750 would have purchased an additional 1,555 shares. Figure 12.2 shows how that would affect your break-even point. By lowering your break-even point to $1.37, when the stock moves back up to $1.75, you have already made a profit of 28 percent!

Most investors make the mistake of putting all their cash into a stock so they don't have anything available to average down when the opportunity presents itself. Even if the investor does have some accessible cash, he or she usually will just invest in another stock rather than take advantage of averaging down and lowering his or her break-even point.

By the way, after Global Marine backed off to that $1.13 price, it turned around and jumped up to $5.75 a share. If you had purchased the original 2,000 shares at $1.75, they would have been worth $11,500. You would have had an $8,000 profit or +229 percent. However, if you had averaged down, you would have 2,555 shares for a value of $14,691. Your profit would have been $11,191 or +320 percent!

Averaging down is the opposite of what most Wall Street brokers would recommend. They prefer to see their clients average up. Using the same example, let's say you bought 1,000 shares of Global Marine at $1.75. The stock moved down to $1.13 and then started back up. It passed $1.75, and when it reached $4, your broker recommended buying more, so your $1,750 balance would purchase an additional 438 shares. You now have 1,438 shares, and if they were sold at the $5.75 price, your total would be $8,269. Your profit would have been $4,769 or 136 percent. This is quite a bit less than what you could have made averaging down. I advise that you only average down. Never average up on your investments.

TAKING ADVANTAGE OF THE NEXT BULL MARKET

Many small investors are missing our current bull market because they follow the crowd. In late 1981 and in 1982, many stocks were extremely underpriced. However, most small investors hesitated to get into the market at that time. Instead, they waited until late 1986 or early 1987 to jump on the bandwagon, at the height of the media hype, when everyone was talking about how much money could be made in stocks. Consequently, those investors bought stocks at extremely high prices, assuming that the stocks would continue to move even higher. Unfortunately, October 19, 1987, dashed those hopes as the market plunged more than 508 points.

A few newsletter writers announced that they had forecast the crash, and many small investors decided "those guys must know what they're doing," so those investors jumped on the writers' bandwagon. Many of the analysts who claimed to have predicted the crash did so because they always were pessimistic. Needless to say, they weren't about to change their strategy because predicting doom had worked before, so everyone ignored the great bargains. The brokerage industry suffered as sales dropped by 50 percent, and the industry had to let many brokers go. This perpetuated the gloomy atmosphere. No one was looking at what the stocks were doing! Figure 12.3 shows the drastic drop in the number of small investors after the crash.

When I wrote the original edition of this book in 1991, my economic models indicated a strong market led by small stocks. Many analysts and the media in general have misforecast this market due to the much publicized downsizing of major corporations. They are just beginning to realize that the true job creators in today's economy are the small to mid-sized companies, not the Fortune 100 companies. For this reason, small stocks have far outpaced the blue chips over the last three years.

Six years after the 1987 crash, many small investors have learned that those bearish newsletter writers caused them to miss out on the

Figure 12.3   Plunge in Number of Small Investors after the Crash

Small Investors Increase Buying Plans...
Percent of holders planning to buy more stock soon

Source: Sindlinger & Co.

greatest bull market in our history. Make sure you're not one of those investors. By investing in quality, low-priced stocks, you'll be positioned to take advantage of the next upswing in the market.

CHAPTER

13

How and When To Sell Your Stock

While no one *knows* the lowest price a stock will hit before it begins to move upward or the highest price it will achieve before starting to fall, the smart investor can use certain techniques to help buy or sell a stock at the best price. This chapter gives you some guideposts for obtaining a good profit.

"Cutting your losses" is a phrase that is commonly used by many Wall Street brokers, analysts and newsletter writers. They advise that if your stock price falls 10 to 20 percent, sell the stock to cut your losses. One well-known adviser recommends selling if your stock falls 8 percent. I believe this advice can be foolish because many volatile stocks can easily fall more than that before soaring upward. If your stock price falls, you should take the time to review the company to learn whether there has been any negative news that caused the price to drop. Sometimes if an investor sells a large block of stock (perhaps he or she lost his job and needed the cash), this can send the stock price tumbling even though the company is still in excellent financial shape. If there doesn't seem to be any valid reason for the decline in the stock price and it has dropped 25 to 30 percent, you may be wiser to average down. (See Chapter 12 for more on averaging down.)

A few years ago I watched Allwaste Corporation, which was recommended at $5.13, move down to $3.75, falling $1 in just one day. Several people called me and said that they had sold near $3.75

"before it went even lower." I just shook my head because the company really didn't have anything wrong with it. In fact, when I called the company to find out why it fell $1 in a day, I learned that an institution sold 300,000 shares at $3.75 (that it bought at $17 per share) just to get out of the stock. Within the next week Allwaste had turned around and shot up to over $6. I'm sure those investors who got frightened and sold at $3.75 kicked themselves because they missed out on an excellent profit opportunity.

TAKING YOUR PROFIT, PROTECTING YOUR PROFIT

A common investment fault is falling in love with your stock and never selling it. For example, the investor watches her stock price rise to the point where she has a good profit. However, she doesn't sell; instead, she watches the stock price fall back down again. The investor has forgotten that the main reason for buying a company's stock is to *make a profit!*

It's all right to love your company, but look at it another way. If you love the company so much, wouldn't you want to own more of it? You can if you are willing to sell when you have a profit and buy it back after the price falls.

If you have $2,000 and like a stock that is selling at $1, you can buy 2,000 shares. If the stock goes up to $3 and you sell, you now have a profit of $4,000 plus your original $2,000. Keep following the stock as it falls back down again to $1.25. After reanalyzing the company to make sure that it still is a good investment, you can buy 4,800 shares with your $6,000. Let's say the company's stock continues on its upward cycle and hits $2.50. You sell the stock and now have $12,000, which gives you a $10,000 or +500 percent profit and allows you to purchase even more shares of stock when the price again falls near its low. You can love a stock, but don't let it blind you to making a profit.

Perhaps one of the most important things to remember when figuring your profit on an investment is to look at the price move in percentages rather than in points. If you don't, you can easily get confused. For example, you have $3,500 to invest and buy $1,500 of stock A, which is selling at $2 per share, and $2,000 worth of stock B, which costs $40 a share. You would be able to buy 750 shares of stock A and 50 shares of stock B.

$1,500 ÷ $2 per share for stock A = 750 shares
$2,000 ÷ $40 per share for stock B = 50 shares

If stock A goes up $.75 and stock B increases by $5, offhand it looks like stock B has performed better. However, if you actually figure out the profit percent, you will see a different story:

750 shares × $.75 increase = $562.50 profit
$562.50 profit ÷ $1,500 purchase price = 38 percent
50 shares × $5 increase = $250 profit
$250 profit ÷ $2,000 purchase price = 13 percent

This example shows why it is important to look at your profits in percentages rather than just in points.

After purchasing a stock, the wise investor will spend a little time along with his or her money and check the stock's price in the local newspaper (if the stock is listed). If the stock hardly moves, checking the price every week may be often enough. However, if the stock is more volatile, it is a good idea to look at its price every day or so. For example, Fonar Corporation had been trading at the $1.50 range for several months and then in two weeks jumped up to $3.59. However, by the end of the following week Fonar had fallen to $2. If the investor didn't check the stock price, she could easily miss the opportunity to make a tidy profit.

Tips for When To Place a Sell Order

From 1982 through 1986 we experienced a runaway bull market, and it was easy to make a 100 percent profit or more on your investments. The market recently has been more volatile, with a slow but steady upward trend. The upward movement of stock prices in general is not as great, and if you have a 50 to 75 percent profit, you might want to take it. Certain telltale signs can indicate the possibility that a stock's price will fall. The smart investor looks for these signs and takes them into consideration.

The Company Announces a Reverse Stock Split

One of the worst decisions a company can make is to execute a reverse stock split. Time and time again, I have seen that maneuver hurt instead of help the stock price. To understand a reverse stock split, you must first learn about a normal stock split.

Figure 13.1   Example of a 3-for-1 Stock Split

100 shares
$15

100 shares
$15

100 shares
$15

Original 100 shares
at $45 per share

100 Shares × $45 per Share = $4,500
300 Shares × $15 per Share = $4,500

Stock Split   A *stock split* occurs when a corporation's board of directors decides that the stock price is too high. Therefore, the company splits the stock and thus the stock price to make it more attractive to institutional buyers and other investors.

Many stock-split configurations are possible: 1.5 for 1; 2 for 1; 3 for 2; 4 for 3; 5 for 1; and 5 for 2 are just a few. How does a stock split work? Figure 13.1 shows a 3-for-1 split. Before the stock split, 100 shares of stock were worth $45 per share. Once the stock is split, the 100 shares become 300 shares, each worth $15. If you multiply the shares by the price, you will see that the dollar value is the same, even though the number of shares is different. Why go through the bother of a stock split? Many companies split their stock to make the price more attractive to investors. The company's total number of outstanding shares also is increased by the stock split. If the company had 2 million shares outstanding before the 3-for-1 stock split, it would have 6 million shares outstanding after the split.

Reverse Stock Split   A *reverse stock split* may occur when a company can't convince any Wall Street analysts or brokers to support its stock. Many times the excuse for the lack of support is that the stock is trading at too low a price. Most Wall Street analysts and brokers

Figure 13.2   Example of a 1-for-8 Reverse Stock Split

	Company		Investor	
	Before	**After**	**Before**	**After**
Shares	32 million	4 million	4,000	500
Price	$1	$8	$1	$8
Value	$32 million	$32 million	$4,000	$4,000

employed at the major brokerage firms will not even review a stock selling below $5. If a company's stock is selling at $1, the company has two choices. It can concentrate on the bottom line, increasing sales and earnings, which should slowly but surely cause the stock price to move upward. *Or* it can take the "quick fix" approach and execute a reverse stock split.

As you have probably guessed from the name, this is just the opposite of a stock split, so instead of ending up with more shares at a lower price, the reverse stock split creates fewer shares at a higher price. For example, if that $1 company has 32 million shares and decides to execute a 1-for-8 reverse split (see Figure 13.2), the company would end up with only 4 million shares at a price of $8 each. Likewise, an investor with 4,000 shares would have 500 shares after the reverse stock split.

In 13 years of recommending stocks I have seen more than 30 companies execute reverse splits, and more than 90 percent of them ended up lower in value than before the reverse split. My statistics show that in almost every case, after a reverse stock split the share-holders' value decreases from 35 to 50 percent or more. Why does this happen? It's simple. One day the stock is selling at $1 per share, and the next day it is selling at $8. There is a resistance factor involved. When a stock's price suddenly jumps up without any substantial gains in profits to bolster the price, the market, which has valued the stock at $1, resists the higher price, causing the price to fall. In addition, many specialists and traders are aware that reverse stock splits cause the price to drop, and they use that to their advantage by shorting the stock, which also applies pressure on the price. Even the small investors help drive the price down. They see that their stock has gone up in price (without realizing that they have proportionately fewer shares), and they sell for a profit (they think). A large amount of "profit taking" can send the stock price tumbling, causing more selling.

This is true whether a company is listed on the pink sheets with no sales and earnings or is an extremely profitable company listed on the NYSE. Navistar International is a prime example. NYSE-listed Navistar is extremely profitable, with more than $4 billion in sales, yet it couldn't successfully pull off a reverse stock split! For a six-month period in 1992 I recommended Navistar at $1.88. After the beginning of 1993 the stock moved up to $3.38, where many investors took their profit, especially when the company announced it was planning to do a 1-for-10 reverse stock split. The reverse split was executed in August 1993, and the price has since fallen to $19.25, creating a 43 percent loss in value for the shareholder.

I believe that a reverse stock split should be approached with extreme caution by the companies that are contemplating it and by investors who own or are thinking of buying stock. Over the years I have seen the vast majority of reverse stock splits seriously erode shareholder value, along with damaging the management's credibility. Any time an investor hears that his company is going to execute a reverse stock split, he should consider selling. If he really likes the stock, the investor will probably be able to buy more shares at a much lower price a few months after the split. I have recently seen instances where reverse stock splits have been successful, but they are very rare.

The Company Raises Cash Through an Equity Offering

A company that needs working capital often will raise the money through an equity offering. The company can offer a portion of its equity through issuing additional common stock, preferred stock, rights, warrants, private stock and convertible or junk bonds. However, with each offering, the additional shares will eventually dilute the value of the company's existing shares. When a company completes such a financing, about 90 percent of the time its stock price falls. The larger the financing, the larger the dilution and, correspondingly, the farther the stock price will drop.

When a shareholder receives the quarterly report, he or she should check the amount of cash the company has. A drastic drop in the company's cash can signal trouble for the stock's price. If the company is in a cash-intensive industry such as the entertainment or high-technology fields, be very careful if the cash drops below $100,000.

To compare the company's cash position, you will need to refer to its annual or 10-K report. In the report's consolidated balance sheet section, the assets will list cash and will show figures for two or more years. (Sometimes there also will be a cash equivalents column, which shows stocks or other investments. They should be considered as cash when determining the company's cash position.) In the following example the cash has radically decreased.

	1993	1992	1991	1990
Cash	$97,369	$4,680,274	$7,747,321	$10,346,837

These figures indicate that the company has been using about $3 to $4 million in cash each year for working capital. With only $97,369 at the end of 1993, the company will probably need to find a way to supplement its cash. If the company is to survive, it will have to obtain more working capital from sales, a loan *or* an offering of more shares through its investment banker.

If the company chooses to offer more shares, it will dilute the value of the existing shares; this usually will cause the stock price to fall. When the smart investor foresees the need for an offering, he or she can sell the stock. Most of the time, the investor can buy it back later after the additional shares have caused the stock price to fall.

Certain industries are not so cash-intensive, and the company may not need such large cash amounts. Pacer Technology is a fine example of a company that usually averages under $100,000 cash on hand. However, this works for Pacer because the company has virtually no long-term debt and expansion is financed from its increasing sales. Perhaps the best strategy when comparing the cash position in previous years is to look for a drastic decrease. Further research should show if the decrease was caused by an acquisition (which could be very positive for the company) or from other more negative sources. By following the company's cash position, the investor can decide if the company will need to find some method of raising working capital and whether the investor should consider selling his or her shares.

Large Increases in Inventory Occur

While reading the balance sheet, also check the inventory position, especially if the company manufactures products. Many times a huge increase in the company's inventory indicates the start of trouble. When inventory builds up in the warehouse, besides the obvious fact that it isn't bringing in revenues, it also creates a drain in the company's finances for the expenses incurred by the additional inventory financing, warehousing, taxes and insurance. If the company's earnings have also dropped, this could mean serious problems on the horizon, so the investor should consider selling the stock.

A Warrant Is about To Expire

Warrant holders won't exercise the warrant to purchase more shares of the company's stock unless the stock price is higher than the price the warrant offers. Some lower-priced companies that need the additional capital generated from the exercise of the warrants will promote their stock to artificially inflate the stock price above the warrant's exercise price so that investors will exercise the warrants. After the warrant is exercised, however, the stock price usually falls because it was raised to an unreal level, there are now more shares outstanding and the stock value has been diluted.

The Company Merges with Another Company

When one company merges with another, typically the stock price jumps in anticipation of the merger and then comes down to the agreed-on price on the day of the official merger. The interest created by the merger news brings in investors, which raises the price, but after the merger, the interest subsides and so does the stock price.

In addition, combining the two newly merged companies may temporarily cause substantial increases in expenses. Personnel changes, reorganization confusion, etc., can cause disastrous reductions in profitability until the reorganization is completed and new personnel learn their jobs. Often the investor can sell the stock for a higher price just before the merger is completed and then buy it back at a lower price after the merger.

When a merger calls for the shareholders to receive one share of the new company for more than one share of the old, this is actually a disguised reverse stock split. For example, the shareholder must pay three shares of the old stock for one share of the new stock. Reverse stock splits usually are bad news for shareholders, so they should sell. A few months later the investor usually can purchase the stock at a price 35 to 50 percent less.

For example, when Robert Halmi, Inc., merged with Hal Roach Studios, the Halmi shareholders paid 2.5 shares of old stock for 1 share of the new company, which was to sell at $5. Several months after the merger, the stock was at $3 or 40 percent less. After many trials, tribulations and name changes, the stock eventually went into bankruptcy.

Another Company Buys Shares for a Much Lower Price

Normally, if one company buys shares of another company that is doing well, it pays a higher price per share than the current market price. Here's why:

When Homestake Mining bought 1 million shares of Galactic Resources, it paid $8.75 per share even though the stock was then selling at $5. Why didn't Homestake just buy the 1 million shares on the open market if the price was cheaper? If Homestake had tried to buy that many shares, it would have caused the stock price to jump up, perhaps as high as $10 or $11 per share. Instead, Homestake contacted Galactic and worked out an agreement that benefited both companies.

If your stock's management agrees to sell a large number of shares to another company at a price that is well below the market price, beware. A CEO who agrees to sell shares for significantly less than the current price is signaling Wall Street that he or she believes that the company's stock price is too high and the price the other company is paying is a more accurate reflection of what it should be.

If a company with great sales, earnings and growth is selling at $4.75 per share but arranges to sell 2 million of its shares for only $2.25, Wall Street will assume that the company's management thinks that it is worth only $2.25, and the stock will probably fall to that price in the near future. If the other company had purchased the 2 million shares on the open market, the stock price would probably have soared to $10. Any company that sells a large number of shares for a lot less than its market price is simply giving the company away, and this is disastrous for the company's shareholders.

MARKET SELL, LIMIT SELL AND STOP LOSS ORDERS

You invested time and effort to research several stocks to discover a quality company at a low price, and now this has paid off: your stock price has risen 200 percent, and it is time to take your profit. You can call your broker to enter either a market sell order or a limit sell order.

Market Sell Order

The vast majority of all sell orders are *market sell orders.* This type of order offers your shares of stock at the best prevailing price (market price) as soon as possible after the order reaches the exchange floor. This is the quickest way to sell the stock, and unless you are selling a large block, it should be executed that same day.

Limit Sell Order

Investors who want to sell their stock for a particular price would use a *limit sell order.* Very simply, this specifies a price and a time period during which the shares will be offered at that price. The limit order is good only for a day unless the investor requests that it be offered for another time period such as a week, month or "until canceled."

The shares may or may not sell depending on whether anyone wishes to pay the specified price. A limit sell order may be canceled at any time and another entered at a higher or lower price depending on the circumstances.

If you bought ABC company at $1 and find the price has risen to $2, you can call your broker and enter a limit sell order offering your shares at $2.25. However, if the stock has not been sold and in fact, the price has fallen to $1.88, you can call your broker, cancel the sell order at $2.25 and enter a new one at whatever price you want. Because you don't want to lose your profit, you may want to enter a sell order at $1.88 or at the market price.

Stop Loss Order

A smart investor will use a *stop loss order* to protect a profit of 100 percent or more. Ideally, you call your broker and set a certain price at which the stock will automatically be sold if it falls that low. If used correctly, the stop loss order is an excellent tool to protect your profit.

For example, if the ABC Company stock has risen to $2.25, the investor can enter a stop loss order with his or her broker at $1.88. If the stock falls to $1.88, it automatically should be sold. If the ABC Company's stock price continues to move upward, the investor would also raise the price at which the stop loss is set.

There is a technique to using the stop loss order. Remember, this is set to protect your profits. You don't really want to sell the stock because you believe it will continue to move upward; however, if it does start to fall, you won't end up back where you started (or worse).

Most stocks don't move straight up or straight down. In its upward cycle a stock may rise ⅜, fall ¼, rise ½ and fall ⅛. The stop loss order has to allow some room for normal downward movement of the stock before it begins to rise again. In many instances the even-dollar price ($2, $3, $4, etc.) becomes a base as the stock falls back that far and then starts upward. Therefore a stop loss order should never be entered at an even-dollar amount. That is why in the previous example the stop loss was set at $1.88 rather than at $2.

As you can see, it becomes a delicate balancing act to try to preserve as much profit as possible if the stock does plunge; however, you also don't want the stop loss price so close to the current stock price that the stock is sold just because the price dipped down before rising again. If the stock is especially volatile, the stop loss may need to be set slightly lower. Once the ABC Company's stock rises to $2.75, the investor would raise the stop loss to $2.38. Avoid the $.50 level, for the stock could easily fall that far. Figure 13.3 shows suggested guidelines for setting a stop loss price for a stock as it rises from $1.

It is possible that your broker cannot handle stop loss orders. Most discount brokers don't offer this service. Also, if the stock is on the Nasdaq market, your broker may be unable to enter a stop loss. If you encounter this problem, you still can make use of this technique by setting your own stop loss point and entering a sell order with your broker if the stock falls to that point. You will have to closely follow the stock price; however, this is worth the effort to avoid losing a good profit.

Don't confuse a stop loss order and a stop limit order. The stop loss order protects the investor's profit by selling the stock if it goes down in price. The stop limit order sets a high price at which the stock will be sold if and when it reaches that price sometime in the future. In addition, the stop loss price is lower than the current market price, while the stop limit price is higher.

TAX SELLING AND THE JANUARY EFFECT

As the end of each year approaches, many brokers recommend that their clients check their portfolios to determine whether they have any stocks that are in a paper-loss position. (The stock's current price is lower than the price at which the stock was purchased.) If so, the

Figure 13.3 Setting a Stop Loss Price

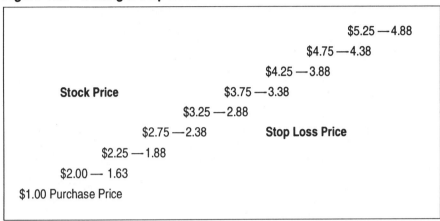

brokers advise their clients to sell the stock and take the loss for tax purposes. This is called a *tax selling strategy.*

I disagree with the timing of that philosophy. Statistics show that most low-priced stocks are closer to their 52-week low price in November and December (probably due to other investors selling for a tax loss and driving down the price). Therefore, because the investor can sell for a tax loss at any time during the year, he would be much wiser to sell at the point that he determines that the investment has become unprofitable.

I believe that the investor shouldn't indiscriminately sell a stock for a tax loss without analyzing it first. Because low-priced stocks seem especially susceptible to the end-of-the-year falling price, if the company is a good investment and the price has just dropped, the wise investor should buy more shares rather than sell for a loss.

One thing to consider when selling stock for a tax loss is that if you are in the 28 percent tax bracket and you sell a stock in late December for a $1,000 loss, you save only $280 in tax dollars. If the stock was a bad investment, fine—$280 is better than nothing. However, if the stock is a quality company, it could easily rise higher than the $280 tax credit after the beginning of the year. For example, Fonar Corporation hit a low of $1.13 in December 1992 primarily because of tax selling. It soared up to $2.59 or +130 percent in January 1993. Investors who held on at the low price made more money than those who sold and received at most a 28 percent tax loss.

Tax selling causes the price of many stocks to drop. When other investors see the price of their stock falling, they panic and sell, causing the price to fall further and creating some excellent bargains. The individuals who sold for the tax loss now have money to invest. However, they wait until after the first of the year for tax purposes, which generates a corresponding upswing in price in January. This phenomenon, called the January Effect, normally results in low-priced stocks far outpacing blue chip stocks.

Smart investors don't follow the crowd; instead, they are contrarians. They use the January Effect to their advantage and buy good-quality, lower-priced stock in early December when the prices have dropped and sell in January or February for a good profit. Using the contrarian approach at any point can be very profitable.

☐   **RULE 10**   ☐

Buy your stock when no one wants it, and sell it when everyone wants to buy.

This approach to investing is just another way of saying "buy low and sell high." A stock's price is determined by supply and demand. That is, if more people want to buy a stock than there are shares available from people who want to sell, the stock price will rise. Likewise, if more people want to sell the stock than there are buyers for it, the stock price will fall. If you invest contrary to the masses, you will buy your quality stock while there is little demand for it and the price is low. Then when other investors become interested in the stock and the price increases, you will sell it for a profit.

CHAPTER

14

Economics and the Stock Market

When I wrote the first edition of this book in the beginning of 1991, I was very bullish and predicted in my newsletter that small stocks would lead a record-breaking market. Over the next three years the market and small stocks soared.

However, the vast majority of analysts and the media were predicting a bearish market for this time period. I believe that they were misled because they still believed that the Fortune 100 companies were the locomotive that runs our economy. Since the majority of these companies were downsizing, laying off tens of thousands of employees, those analysts painted a gloomy picture for the market. Every time General Motors or DuPont announced a cutback, the media would have a field day. "Woe is us . . . The economy is sick . . . Just look at all those huge conglomerates letting all those people go." We even elected our president on the false assumption that we were experiencing the worst economy in 50 years. These outlandish statements were backed up by equally outlandish theories and statistics.

Of course, the day after the media's choice, Bill Clinton, got the job, our economy magically turned around. How did this happen? It occurred because those analysts had ignored the *true* job creators—small industry. In addition, the massive cutbacks were not as bad as the media indicated because the majority of employees were given the option of early retirement or jobs lost to attrition were just not filled.

Thousands of workers didn't suddenly find themselves out on the street as the media would have us believe. Once the media had something to be happy about (their man got elected), the positive economic indicators that had been disregarded before were now getting reported. With the optimistic viewpoint now bombarding us, consumer confidence rebounded almost overnight. It's a great example of the self-fulfilling prophecy and shows that you can't always trust the analysts to really know what's going on.

WHAT MAKES THE MARKET MOVE?

The U.S. economic condition is one of the more important factors affecting the direction in which the stock market moves. Perhaps the best example of this is the stock market crash on October 19, 1987. On that day the market closed down 508 points. That was the largest move in history and was a much greater plunge than Black Friday in 1929, which heralded the Great Depression. From the time the market closed on October 19th until it reopened on October 20th, virtually every stock market analyst and economist predicted how bad the market would be on the 20th. Many anticipated that the crash would bring on a depression as Black Friday did. They were wrong. The U.S. economy was strong, and instead of the stock market crash affecting the economy, the economy affected the stock market. On October 20th, the market experienced a 103-point rally, which was the second largest stock movement in history!

Throughout November and December the fallout continued as the "doom-and-gloom" market analysts speculated that retailers were going to be badly hurt by the crash. Predictions were running the gamut from a slight recession to a full-blown depression. I disagreed with those analysts. The economic statistics just weren't that bad; in fact, they were pretty good. As the months passed, it became apparent that there wouldn't be a depression, not even a true recession. The Dow rebounded to its precrash record highs and surpassed them, breaking 3,000 in June 1990 and 3,800 in January 1994.

Why was *The CHEAP Investor* right and so many analysts with all their fancy computer programs, charts and expensive equipment wrong? Most analysts evidently were assuming that the stock market would affect the economy. However, I believed the economic indicators demonstrated an economy that was strong enough to weather the crash.

To understand how the market moves, you must first understand what moves the market. I believe that the *economic indicators,* which are key statistics showing the direction of the economy, can be used to loosely predict market trends. Among the indicators are the gross domestic product (GDP), the consumer price index (CPI), the producer price index (PPI), interest rates, inflation and the unemployment rate.

I am not surprised that historical comparisons of stock indexes and the measures of economic activity, such as the GDP, CPI, PPI and the interest and unemployment rates, indicate a correlation between the direction of stock prices and the general state of the economy.

This chapter will explain each of the major economic indicators, show how they have performed over the past several years and demonstrate what effect the indicators have on the economy in general and on the stock market in particular.

THE GROSS DOMESTIC PRODUCT (GDP)

Formerly called the gross national product, the *gross domestic product* (GDP) growth rate is the primary indicator of the status of the economy. Figures on the GDP are released every quarter. It measures the activity and market prices of all goods and services produced during the year. It is the value of goods and services bought and sold, including consumer consumption, investment in business equipment, foreign investment in the United States and government purchases. (See Figure 14.1.)

There are two basic ways to measure the GDP. The first is the flow-of-income approach. Households provide business firms with resources (labor, entrepreneurial ability, property, etc.). For those resources businesses pay rent, wages and salaries, interest and profits to members of the households. If all the resource payments were added up, they would make up the national income. Combining indirect taxes collected by the government (mostly property and sales taxes) and depreciation allowances (found on the tax returns of business firms) with the national income creates the GDP.

Another method of measuring the GDP uses expenditures, adding all the money spent by individual consumers, business firms and the government. For example, consumers receive income from businesses in return for their labor, property, etc. Then the money the consumers receive flows back to various firms in exchange for goods and services. The money circulates as more goods are produced and

Figure 14.1   Gross Domestic Product (GDP)

paid for and more individuals are hired to produce the goods. If business investment expenditures and government expenditures are added to the consumer expenditures previously described, the total is the GDP.

Comparing the GDP from one year to the next can be misleading. If, for example, the GDP increased from $4 trillion to $4.4 trillion, the GDP would appear to have done quite well, increasing by 10 percent. However, before we celebrate we must remember that the GDP measured all the goods and services produced that year *at market prices*. If, because of inflation, prices rose 10 percent that year, we actually are just breaking even. Because inflated prices can make the GDP rise while actual production has remained the same, the *real GDP* was devised to take inflation into account and give a more accurate picture of our growth. (See Figure 14.2.)

The GDP is extremely important, for it reveals the condition of our economic system. Figure 14.3 shows our real GDP changes for the past several years.

The GDP indicates the direction in which the country is headed. The optimum growth percentage is between 2.5 and 3.5 percent. Once the economy starts growing more than 4 percent, it may become inflationary, causing interest rates to rise, and that can be disastrous to the stock market.

Figure 14.2   Real Gross Domestic Product

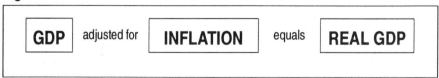

Figure 14.3   Real Gross Domestic Product since 1982

Year	Percent	Year	Percent	Year	Percent
1982	−2.2	1986	2.9	1990	1.2
1983	3.9	1987	3.1	1991	−0.7
1984	6.2	1988	3.9	1992	2.6
1985	3.2	1989	2.5	1993	2.9

THE CONSUMER PRICE INDEX (CPI)

The *consumer price index* (CPI) measures change in consumer prices determined from a monthly survey tabulated by the U.S. Bureau of Labor Statistics. The survey is designed to compare price changes in goods and services over a period of time and is based on a sample of prices in seven major categories—food and beverages, housing, apparel and upkeep, transportation, medical care, entertainment and other goods and services.

The CPI also is known as the cost-of-living index, which is important to millions of people who receive cost-of-living pay increases. That group includes Social Security beneficiaries, retired military and government employees, food stamp recipients and workers covered by collective-bargaining agreements.

Since 1974, when the CPI hit double digits, there has been wide interest by the media, financial community, unions, employees and retirees who want to know whether they are keeping up or falling behind when comparing what we earn with what we have to spend. The bureau chose 1967 as the CPI's base year and assigned it an index number of 100. Prices for other years are reported from this base.

Example: In 1993 it took over $400 to purchase the same $100 worth of goods and services in 1967.

Each month the Bureau of Labor Statistics buys a fixed sample market basket of goods and services from the seven categories. To reflect changes in consumer spending, the market basket, which determines the CPI, is revised every few years. Figure 14.4 shows the major yearly changes in the CPI.

The high percentage jumps in the CPI in 1974, 1975, 1979, 1980, 1981 and 1990 were caused by dramatically increased oil prices. High

Figure 14.4   Consumer Price Index Yearly Changes from 1967

Year	Percent	Year	Percent	Year	Percent
1967	2.9	1976	5.8	1985	3.8
1968	4.2	1977	6.5	1986	1.1
1969	5.4	1978	7.7	1987	4.4
1970	5.9	1979	13.3	1988	4.4
1971	4.3	1980	13.5	1989	4.6
1972	3.3	1981	10.3	1990	6.1
1973	6.2	1982	6.2	1991	3.1
1974	11.0	1983	3.2	1992	2.9
1975	9.1	1984	3.9	1993	2.7

oil prices had profound consequences on financial markets world-wide.

The CPI reflects the inflation rate. It is very significant to the financial markets because if prices increase by a high rate, it raises the amount of money the government must pay to accomplish its job, which increases the budget deficit. If the budget deficit expands too fast, it has a disastrous effect on the financial markets and could cause them to crash. Over the years analysts have found that a CPI of 3 to 4.5 percent sustains our economic health. A figure of more than 6 percent generally is considered inflationary.

THE PRODUCER PRICE INDEX (PPI)

Formerly called the wholesale price index, the *producer price index* (PPI) measures changes in the wholesale prices of products and services. It is calculated and released on a monthly basis by the U.S. Bureau of Labor Statistics. Prices are measured as products move through the manufacturing and distribution stages of our economy to the consumer. The index is broken down into the components of commodity, industry, sector and stage of processing. Figure 14.5 indicates the PPI changes from 1967 to 1993.

The PPI is probably the most accurate reflection of the change in wholesale inflation. Figure 14.5 shows a dramatic reduction in the PPI changes since 1981.

Figure 14.5   Producer Price Index Yearly Changes from 1967

Year	Percent	Year	Percent	Year	Percent
1967	1.0	1976	4.6	1985	1.0
1968	2.8	1977	6.1	1986	−1.4
1969	4.8	1978	7.8	1987	2.1
1970	2.2	1979	12.6	1988	2.5
1971	4.0	1980	11.8	1989	5.2
1972	6.5	1981	7.1	1990	4.9
1973	13.1	1982	3.6	1991	2.1
1974	18.9	1983	1.6	1992	1.2
1975	9.3	1984	2.1	1993	1.8

If the PPI increases, usually six or eight months later those higher prices are reflected as a higher rate in the CPI. Therefore, if the PPI increases by 6 or 7 percent, it may show up several months later as an 8 to 9 percent increase on the CPI.

THE INTEREST RATE

Interest rates fluctuate according to the laws of supply and demand. As the demand for money increases, interest rates rise. As the rates rise, the price of borrowing money becomes too high and the demand for money declines. When less money is borrowed, the supply of available money expands, and interest rates fall as the supply of funds exceeds the demand for funds at the current rates.

At lower interest rates, business firms borrow more for investment purposes (such as building a new facility or expanding into a new market). Why? Because at a very high interest rate, few investment projects are worthwhile. However, as the interest rate declines, more and more investment projects become feasible.

Discount Rate and Prime Rate

Two major indicators show the direction of interest rates—the discount rate and the prime rate. The *discount rate* is the rate of interest charged by the central bank of the Federal Reserve System to member banks who borrow and pledge securities or other assets for collateral.

Figure 14.6   Discount Rate since 1970

Year	High	Low	Year	High	Low	Year	High	Low
1970	6.0	5.5	1978	9.5	6.0	1986	7.5	5.5
1971	5.0	4.5	1979	12.0	9.5	1987	6.0	5.5
1972	4.5	4.5	1980	13.0	10.0	1988	6.5	6.0
1973	7.5	4.5	1981	14.0	12.0	1989	7.0	7.0
1974	8.0	7.75	1982	12.0	8.5	1990	7.0	6.5
1975	7.8	6.0	1983	8.5	8.5	1991	5.5	3.25
1976	6.0	5.25	1984	9.0	8.0	1992	3.25	3.0
1977	6.0	5.25	1985	8.0	7.5	1993	3.0	3.0

(See Figure 14.6.) It provides a floor for interest rates. Member banks would not charge customers an interest rate below the discount rate, for that is the interest rate the member bank has to pay.

As the discount rate is either raised or lowered, it influences the *prime rate,* which is the lowest interest rate a commercial bank will charge its preferred customers for short-term, unsecured debts. (See Figure 14.7.)

The discount and prime rates are significant to the consumer, business and government because they determine the direction that general interest rates move. Any time the prime rate or discount rate is adjusted, it is reported in the business section of newspapers across the country.

Interest rates are regulated by the Federal Reserve Board, a government agency that controls the amount of money that flows through our economic system. The Federal Reserve Board is responsible for setting interest rate trends by adjusting the discount rate.

When the Federal Reserve Board raises the discount rate, its member banks in turn raise their interest rates since it now costs them more to borrow. On the other hand, if the Federal Reserve Board lowers the discount rate, its member banks usually lower their interest rates accordingly.

The Federal Reserve Board also determines reserve requirements for banks, and this changes the amount of money a bank can lend. By loosening or tightening the supply of money a bank can lend, the board can help regulate the economy. In addition, the Federal Reserve Board directly controls margin requirements, which affect both large and small investors.

Interest rates are extremely important to the economy. Just about everyone borrows money. The rates affect the consumer in the form

Figure 14.7 Prime Rate since 1970

Year	High	Low	Year	High	Low	Year	High	Low
1970	8.5	6.75	1978	11.75	7.75	1986	9.0	7.5
1971	6.75	5.25	1979	15.75	11.5	1987	9.75	8.0
1972	6.0	5.0	1980	21.5	10.75	1988	10.5	8.5
1973	10.0	6.0	1981	20.5	15.75	1989	11.0	10.0
1974	12.0	9.75	1982	17.0	11.5	1990	10.0	10.0
1975	10.5	7.0	1983	11.5	10.5	1991	10.0	8.5
1976	7.25	6.25	1984	13.0	10.75	1992	8.5	6.25
1977	7.75	6.25	1985	10.75	9.5	1993	6.0	6.0

of mortgages, automobile and personal loans, credit-card finance charges and home-equity loans. Both small and large businesses must borrow money for expansion, inventory financing, day-to-day expenses and many other reasons. The government borrows to continue serving U.S. citizens through a multitude of programs. The Federal Reserve Board walks a tightrope between allowing too much borrowing, which becomes inflationary, and not permitting enough borrowing, which can cause a recession as consumers and businesses reduce spending; this in turn spirals into further spending cuts.

How Are Interest Rates Related to the Stock Market?

There is a tremendous conflict of opinion on interest rates. I believe that if you note any major long-term trend in interest rates, the opposite trend will affect the stock market. For example, those who guessed or predicted that interest rates would drop drastically from a prime rate of 10 percent in 1990 to a little over half that rate in four years could also have predicted that the stock market would soar.

In general, if you compare the longer-term trends in interest rate movements and the stock market, you will observe a correlation between the two. If interest rates move up, the stock market normally will move down and vice versa. However, when interest rates are adjusted just a half point up or down, this probably will not have much influence on the market.

Another viewpoint is that when the prime rate fluctuates between 6 and 11 percent, companies and investors usually are interested in borrowing money. However, once the prime rate hits 12 percent or

Figure 14.8   Effect of Rising Oil Prices on Monthly Inflation from April 1990 to December 1990

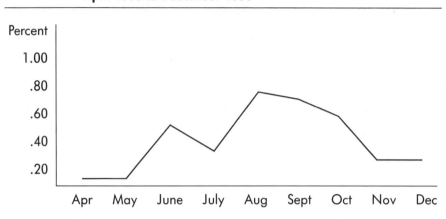

higher, they hesitate to borrow, which slows expansion and investment.

INFLATION

Like death and taxes, inflation seems to be unavoidable. In many cases it is self-perpetuating. As consumers see prices rising and reasonably assume that prices will continue to do so, they rush out to buy more goods and services before prices climb even higher. When businesses see that by increasing prices they actually help their sales, they are encouraged to continue the trend by raising prices again. Inflation is an economic environment in which prices rise, resulting in a decline in the dollar's buying power.

Inflation can be caused by several different situations. When there is more demand for goods and services than can be produced, prices will increase. Because wages constitute the majority of the cost of doing business, any significant wage increase must be passed along to consumers in the form of higher prices. These increased prices raise everyone's cost of living, creating a demand for further wage increases. The inflation rates are reflected by the CPI, as shown previously in Figure 14.4.

Inflation also can be caused by supply-side cost shocks. In 1990, oil prices soared from $17 per barrel in July to more than $40 in September due to concerns about oil shortages caused by the Iraqi invasion and occupation of Kuwait. (See to Figure 14.8.) In this case there was no shortage; in fact, there was an oversupply of oil. There- fore, once the panic subsided, oil prices and the inflation rate dropped dramatically in October, November and December.

While a 1 or 2 percent annual increase in the CPI would alarm virtually no one, anything above 6 percent is considered hyperinfla- tion. During a hyperinflationary trend, it becomes increasingly diffi- cult to conduct normal economic activities. Prices constantly climb, and it becomes almost impossible to enter into long-term contracts.

Inflation and interest rates go hand in hand. Because of the regulation by the Federal Reserve Board, if inflation rises too fast, interest rates will be raised to restrain the inflationary trend.

As interest rates rise, the cost of doing business increases, causing even higher inflation, which negatively affects the stock market. As inflation is regulated by higher interest rates and eventually starts to move downward, it spurs the stock market upward.

THE UNEMPLOYMENT RATE

The Bureau of Labor Statistics conducts a random survey of households to compute the unemployment rate. The survey asks these three questions:

1. Are you working?
2. Did you work at all this month—even for one day?
3. Did you look for work during the month?

If an individual answers yes to questions 1 or 2, he or she is classified as employed. If the individual answers yes only to question 3, he or she is considered unemployed. However, if the individual answered no to all three questions, he or she is labeled a "discouraged worker" and does not get counted as unemployed. Figure 14.9 shows the unemployment rate for the past several years.

It is important to follow the unemployment statistics because they can also impact the stock market. Double-digit unemployment is considered negative for the stock market because a large percentage of potential consumers will be restricting their purchases, causing business to slow down. On the other hand, unemployment under 3.5 percent is also negative because it can create a demand greater than the supply of products, which may cause businesses to raise their prices as they pay higher wages to attract more employees to manu-

Figure 14.9   Unemployment Rates from 1980

Year	Percent	Year	Percent	Year	Percent
1980	7.1	1985	7.1	1990	5.4
1981	7.6	1986	6.9	1991	6.6
1982	9.7	1987	6.1	1992	7.3
1983	9.6	1988	5.4	1993	6.4
1984	7.4	1989	5.2		

facture additional products. An unemployment rate between 5 and 7 percent is usually considered good for inflation, interest rates and the market.

While I have gone into great detail explaining some of the prime economic indicators, you don't have to spend hours studying them each month when they are released. A good habit to form, however, would be to glance through the Sunday newspaper's business section each week looking for the release of any indicators and then determine if there is any upward or downward trend. (A trend would be an upward or downward movement that has continued for at least three or four months.)

Once you have pinpointed a trend, you can take it into consideration when reviewing your portfolio. If you have followed my advice in choosing quality, low-priced stocks, your main concern would be whether or not to take a profit in your investments if you detect a trend that could have a negative impact on the stock market.

CHAPTER

15

Profiting from Volatility

At one time an investor could purchase a quality stock, put it in a safe-deposit box and forget about it while it grew over the years into a nice nest egg for retirement. Unfortunately, that is not true today. Technology has changed the playing rules of investments. Instead of putting your stock away and letting it grow, today's money is made by actively trading stocks. The vast majority of stocks are cyclical, and smart investors can make much more by purchasing a stock near its 52-week low and selling near its high than by holding it for long-term appreciation.

Up-to-the-minute information about stock prices, markets and indexes is readily available to everyone. In Chicago three TV channels broadcast major investment programs during the hours the market is open. While the programs broadcast news on the latest developments that could affect the market or interview various individuals, the NYSE and AMEX trades are listed at the bottom of the TV screen. In addition, the investor can receive the latest stock-trade prices on a home computer over the telephone line or from a satellite dish or FM receiver.

COMPUTERIZED PROGRAM TRADING

Computers have revolutionized the stock market. Orders to buy and sell stocks, bonds, mutual funds, etc., are transmitted around the world at the speed of light. Computers provide instant confirmation of trades, up-to-the-second quotes for stocks and diverse information that normally would not be easily accessible for the small investor. Not only is computerized information a tremendous asset for the small investor, it is vital to institutions, large brokerage firms and portfolio managers.

Computerized program trading has been spawned by the modern age of high-speed communications and computerized stock trading. Because the trader can react so quickly to market changes, program trading is an invaluable tool that is used and abused. For better or worse, it has totally changed the marketplace, causing tremendous market volatility in a short period of time. Program trading was a major culprit behind the stock market crash of 1987.

A small investor can make huge profits by not panicking when the market is extremely volatile and by taking advantage of swings that cause stock prices to plunge to unrealistic lows. Buying quality stocks that are undervalued can prove extremely profitable.

VOLATILITY—A LEGACY OF THE CRASH OF 1987

I have referred to the 1987 stock market crash several times in this book because we still are feeling repercussions from it today. Stock market volatility became a major issue because of the crash, and restrictions on the amount of upward or downward swings have been put into place to avoid plunges such as the one we experienced then.

On October 19, 1987, the stock market, as measured by the Dow Jones Industrial Average, experienced the largest single-day movement in its history. Unfortunately, the movement was down—508 points or about 22 percent. This disastrous plunge caused widespread panic. Stock market analysts and economic experts predicted a great depression or at least a major recession for 1988. This didn't happen.

What caused the crash of 1987? The day after the 508-point plunge, I wrote the following in an editorial for *The CHEAP Investor:*

> We believe the blue chip stocks were at record high prices because of *greed*. Most were extremely overpriced, and then institutional buyers (who own a large percentage of blue chips)

panicked and sold all day Monday (October 19th), causing a 22 percent drop in the Dow.

By Tuesday, those embarrassed institutional buyers realized that the blue chips were now at unrealistically low prices and began buying them back. . . . There is no doubt that what happened the week of October 19, 1987, will be remembered for the rest of our lives. Since investments are measured over a long period of time in peaks and valleys, hopefully we can look back at this valley as a great investment opportunity.

For the next couple of months after the crash, most of the "experts" were still predicting various forms of doom for our economy. They felt that the retailers would experience a very gloomy holiday season as most consumers would buy less-expensive gifts and entertain more economically. I disagreed. The economic indicators were all positive, and while many investors had the breath knocked out of them, I didn't think the crash was going to have that drastic an effect on the economy. The 1987 holiday season far exceeded the analysts' expectations.

The crash of 1987 created a lot of good buys—good-bye Jaguar, good-bye yacht, good-bye high lifestyle. Seriously, it affected a lot of lives but not so many and not as drastically as the analysts had predicted.

Events Leading to the Crash

To see the buildup of the crash potential, we'll go back in history to 1986, when the consensus was that we were experiencing the greatest bull market in our history. Wall Street analysts, institutions and individual investors started to buy virtually any stock or mutual fund at record high prices, assuming prices would continue to move higher. At the end of 1986 we saw the Dow close at 1,896. Practically every day newspapers, magazines and TV newscasts headlined one broken Wall Street record after another. Everywhere you looked, you were bombarded with the wonderful news of how well the stock market was doing and how everyone was making lots of money. Needless to say, those who hadn't already invested wanted to join the crowd because they didn't want to miss out on a "sure thing."

On January 9, 1987, the market had skyrocketed through the 2,000 level, and the media increased its coverage on the record-setting stock market. Foreign money was being invested in blue chips and mutual funds at record levels, and the stock market continued its upward movement, closing the end of January at 2,163. Despite the continued upward record-setting movement, I started to see some signals of change. The trade deficit began to capture the media's attention as it hit a record monthly high on January 2, 1987, at $19.22 billion. Interest rates, inflation and other economic indicators hit bottom in 1986 and were showing signs of moving up. Oil prices hit an 11-month high, closing at $18 a barrel the first week in January 1987. These indicators spurred me to write an editorial in January 1987 that predicted a bullish 1987 for just the first six months. I was concerned that the increasing oil prices, interest and inflation rates and deficit could come back to haunt us.

A big factor for the January 1987 huge upward thrust in the market was a *Barron's* article quoting a self-proclaimed Wall Street guru. The "guru" predicted that the Dow would hit 3,600, and the day the article was printed, the Dow claimed a new one-day jump record of 44 points. On January 22d the Dow soared 51 points. The excitement continued in February as the Dow shot up 54 points to 2,238 on the 17th due to foreign buying and something called program trading. February closed at 2,224.

In early March Jim Wright, the Democratic Speaker of the House, announced that he was working toward a goal of raising taxes by about $20 billion a year. The Dow moved down in reaction to the announcement, but by the end of March was at 2,305. In April interest rates started to move up, surprising Wall Street and inflicting large losses on the bond debts of securities firms. The month closed down at 2,286. With the trade debt increasing, Congress tried to fix the problem with the Gephardt amendment, which called for major protectionist legislation. The financial markets shuddered at the prospect. The bill lost 218 to 214. The market closed at 2,297.

On June 3d, Paul Volker resigned as chairman of the Federal Reserve Board, and Alan Greenspan, a Volker clone, was nominated to take his place. Again the market shuddered and the dollar plunged. However, as the GDP indicators continued to increase, the dollar rebounded, and the market started moving up again, closing in June at 2,418. In July the major indicators continued to rise, and *The Wall Street Journal* wrote that economic expansion would last at least another year. The market continued to soar and then ticked downward when the Senate passed legislation calling for action against countries with a "consistent pattern of import barriers" (i.e., Japan). By mid-July strong foreign buying and computerized program trading moved the market upward, so July closed at 2,572.

In the beginning of August oil prices began to tumble, sparking a rally in the stock market. On August 11th the market broke 2,600, and two days later it was at 2,680. As the media blitz about the amazing market grew, individuals who didn't want to miss "the opportunity to make money" bought just about anything at record-high prices. On August 25th the market hit an all-time high of 2,746.65 but closed at 2,722.42. IBM hit a high of 174 and fell, as analysts reduced the company's 1987 earnings estimates. Other major stocks followed the downward movement. The trade deficit widened to a new record of $39.53 billion in the second quarter, causing the market to continue its fall. August closed at 2,662.95.

Early in September oil prices moved up to near $20, and on September 3d, the Federal Reserve Board raised the discount rate from 5.5 percent to 6.5 percent. The prime rate rose from 8.25 percent to 8.75 percent. The dollar plunged, causing the stock market to fall to 2,549 by September 9th. Several major analysts concluded that 2,549 would be the low point. Meanwhile, the Wall Street guru continued to be bullish, never losing faith that the Dow would hit 3,600 before the next bear market. The market seesawed, closing at 2,596 in September.

By October 13th the market was down to 2,508. The next day the guru had a change of heart and revised his outlook to include a 300-point drop in the Dow before it rose to 3,600. The Dow plunged 91 points. Congress was having trouble meeting the Gramm-Rudman budget reduction targets and put a $12 billion tax package together. Troubles continued with the trade deficit and the value of the dollar. An American-registered tanker was hit in Kuwaiti waters, causing oil prices to soar. These factors all contributed to the 260-point drop between October 14th and 16th. When the market closed Friday, October 16th, it stood at 2,246, primarily because of mass selling by institutional buyers through portfolio selling and computerized sell programs.

Program trading accounted for a stunning 43 percent of the NYSE total volume. During the last half hour the selling hysteria reached such a magnitude that it was destined to continue on Monday. Instead of being a cooling-off period, the weekend of October 17th and 18th intensified the bearish attitude.

The Day of the Crash

On October 19th the stock market experienced its now famous plunge. Friday's needless computer-driven program trading by institutions would continue with force that Monday. What may have been prudent selling on Friday had turned into wholesale desertion over the weekend.

The year 1987 was the year of the mutual fund as institutional and individual investors bought mutual funds at record-high prices, assuming they would continue to move upward. The Fidelity group of mutual funds was considered king, and when Fidelity bought a stock, Wall Street would follow. One of the big sellers on the morning of October 19th would be Fidelity, which offered to sell more than $1 billion in assets, and of course, everyone followed.

As the day began, overseas markets plunged: London was down 22 percent; Tokyo, 17 percent; Zurich, 14 percent; Frankfurt, 13 percent; Hong Kong, 11 percent; and Singapore, 33 percent. More bad news hit the wires at 7:00 A.M. EST when it was announced that the United States had leveled two Iranian oil platforms. This seemed to fuel the mass selling orders of foreign and institutional investors.

To address the situation before the opening of the New York Stock Exchange, NYSE Chairman John Pheian said, "The way to make sure stocks open well in volatile markets is don't open them quickly." This backfired and caused more panic selling. In fact, the later a stock opened, the lower was its opening price.

Figure 15.1 shows the Friday closing prices of the 30 Dow Industrial stocks and their opening prices on Monday morning. Every stock opened lower than it closed on Friday, and most continued to fall during the day because of the herd instinct and the computerized selling of institutions.

When the market opened at 9:30 A.M. EST, the stock index futures plunged, causing the Dow to drop 50 points almost immediately. (See Figure 15.2.) In addition, the delay in opening hundreds of stocks caused more anxiety and worsened the situation. The selling pressure was so severe that by 11:00 A.M. all but one of the Dow 30 stocks had opened, and the Dow had moved down more than 200 points to 2,025. In a correction, the market moved up slightly to 2,125 by 12:00 noon.

However, major margin calls for takeover stocks caused the market to move back down to 2,050 by 1:00 P.M. With rumors abounding that the SEC and the exchanges were considering closing the markets, the Dow continued down to about 1,975 by 2:00 P.M. A small correction showed 2,000 at 2:45 P.M., and then panic reigned. Headed by

Figure 15.1 Dow Jones Industrials Stock Change (October 19, 1987)

Close 10-16-87	Company Name	Open 10-19-87	Close 10-19-87	Points Down
56.00	Alcoa	51.00	42.50	13.50
39.13	Allied Signal	35.50	27.63	11.50
30.00	AT&T	28.38	23.63	6.38
16.50	Bethlehem Steel	15.75	11.00	5.50
43.63	Boeing	41.88	38.50	5.13
49.50	Chevron	47.50	41.25	8.25
40.50	Coca-Cola	36.25	30.50	10.00
98.50	DuPont	90.00	80.50	18.00
43.75	Exxon	40.00	33.50	10.25
50.75	General Electric	42.00	41.88	8.88
66.00	General Motors	65.38	60.00	6.00
59.50	Goodyear Tire	53.00	42.50	17.00
135.00	IBM	122.00	103.25	31.75
46.38	International Paper	41.00	33.88	12.50
90.13	Kodak	75.63	62.88	27.25
43.63	McDonald's	40.50	36.38	7.25
184.00	Merck	162.00	160.00	24.00
70.25	Minnesota Mining	64.00	56.00	14.25
6.00	Navistar International	5.88	4.88	1.13
102.75	Philip Morris	90.00	88.13	14.63
44.38	Primerica	41.38	34.13	10.25
85.00	Procter & Gamble	82.00	61.38	23.63
41.50	Sears, Roebuck	36.75	31.00	10.50
36.50	Texaco	32.00	32.00	4.50
27.38	Union Carbide	26.25	24.75	2.63
48.63	United Tech.	46.50	41.00	7.63
34.00	USX Corp.	32.25	21.50	12.50
60.50	Westinghouse	51.00	40.25	20.25
42.50	Woolworth	41.25	36.50	6.00

Figure 15.2 The October 19, 1987, Crash

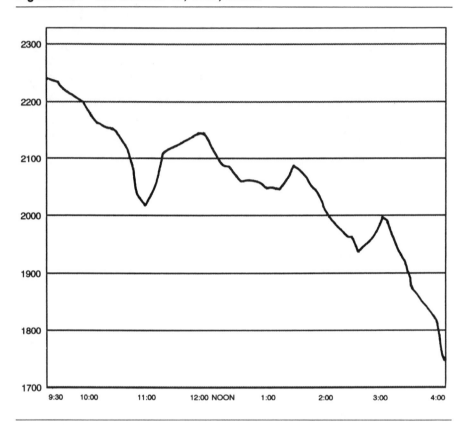

computerized sell programs, institutions, mutual funds, foreign and individual sellers started to sell at any price. They got their wish, and the market plunged from 2,000 to 1,738. The only thing that stopped the hysterical selling was the closing bell.

The result was the worst loss experienced by the stock market in 78 years. The Dow had dropped an incredible 508 points in six and one-half hours. This was a day that everyone in the financial community will remember for the rest of their lives.

The Next Day—A Recovery

On Tuesday, October 20th, the overseas markets were relatively calm despite the fact that several markets were down, including Tokyo, which fell 225 points or about 9 percent; London, which dropped 13 percent; and Frankfurt, which declined 5 percent. Before the market opened on Tuesday, Alan Greenspan, Federal Reserve Board chairman, stated, "The Federal Reserve affirms its readiness to serve as a source of liquidity to support the economic and financial system." This support was probably a major reason why there was a vast number of buy orders by institutions when the market opened, and those orders helped precipitate the market rally. On the 20th the market soared, hitting a high of 2,067 or +325 points, but closed at 1,841 up 103 points.

It was mainly the higher-priced and blue chip stocks that suffered major losses on October 19th; however, October 20th was more disastrous to the small investor. As the media created a Super Bowl atmosphere about the stock market crash, the small investor understandably became more anxious and confused. The 20th saw an influx of sell orders from small investors in lower-priced stocks. In some cases, a vicious cycle was created as the mass selling caused the stock price to decline further, causing more panic selling.

With hindsight, it is easy to look back to see the signs indicating that the bull market we experienced couldn't go on much longer. Using common sense and the economic indicators, you can determine your own investing strategy to take those factors into consideration.

VOLATILITY CAUSED BY THE MIDDLE EAST OIL CRISIS

During mid- to late-1990 investors had the opportunity to profit during the huge drop in the Dow Jones Industrials from 3,034 in June to 2,350 in October. The crisis was caused by the Iraqi invasion of Kuwait on August 2, 1990. The invasion precipitated an almost 700-point drop that occurred over a three-month period as oil prices at the pump were going up. Figure 15.3 shows the 700-point decline.

That 700-point drop was far more devastating than the 500-point drop in 1987 because it was a long-term decline, unlike the 1987 plunge that showed good recovery the next day. The combination of continually falling stock prices and rising gasoline prices crushed investor confidence and kept many from investing in potentially lucrative undervalued stocks. According to the consumer confidence

Figure 15.3   Dow Jones Industrials Plunge during Middle East Oil Crisis

Source: Reprinted by permission of *Barron's*, © 1991 Dow Jones & Company, Inc. All Rights Reserved Worldwide.

index, which hit a high of 82 percent in June, consumer confidence fell to a low of 68 percent at the end of 1990.

The panic resulting from the crisis caused many quality stock prices to plunge to the point where they were very undervalued. Investors who follow the contrarian philosophy realize that this is a great opportunity. It just takes a certain amount of courage to buy your bargain stock when everyone else is selling.

WAYS TO PROFIT FROM VOLATILITY

While major market plunges can create many bargains, volatility in an industry can also affect stock prices. For example, companies that mine gold, silver or platinum usually see their stocks move upward or downward in response to increasing or decreasing prices for their particular commodity.

I like to follow oil prices because many oil stocks are also affected by fluctuations in the price per barrel. For example, in May 1988 the commodity price dropped to $15 per barrel, and oil stocks in general were near their 52-week low prices. I recommended Galveston-Houston at $1.75 per share. Listed on the NYSE, it had experienced hard times but had started to turn its balance sheet around. Over the next year, as the price of crude oil increased, Galveston-Houston's stock soared to more than $7 or +300 percent! Because the price per barrel was still near $15 in August 1988, I recommended Varco International, listed on the NYSE at $3. Its price soon skyrocketed to $13.75 or +358 percent.

However, when oil prices fell in the summer of 1990 to $17 per barrel, the situation was different because many oil companies' stocks were near the high points of their cycles. For example, Galveston-Houston's price was more than $6, and Varco was at $12. When crude oil prices shot up from $17 to more than $40, there were many headlines about the huge profits that were made in oil stocks. Unfortunately, the headlines were misleading because the individuals who wrote those articles assumed that most oil stocks soared as oil commodity prices rose. That didn't happen because those writers didn't realize that two conditions are necessary for oil stock prices to jump when oil commodity prices shoot up. Not only should the price per barrel be low; the quality oil companies' stocks should be near their 52-week low price. The best way to ensure a profit is to find a stock that meets both requirements.

At the beginning of 1994 oil prices have again plunged to a five-year low of $13. Many Wall Street analysts are excitedly hyping their favorite overpriced oil stocks, but investors who get sucked in will more than likely lose. Why? Despite low commodity prices, most oil stocks are not at their low points. For instance, quality stocks such as Global Marine (NYSE–GLM) is selling at $4.50, and Varco International (NYSE–VRC) is at $6.25, while their 52-week lows are $2.13 and $4.13 respectively. Unit Corporation's (NYSE–UNT) low is $1.63, yet the stock is selling at $3.25; Energy Services' (AMEX–ESV) low is $.88, while it is trading at $3.25.

When volatility causes stock prices in a particular industry to fall, don't be so overwhelmed by "bargains" that you forget to completely analyze the company. Make sure that it meets the normal requirements of price—near the 52-week low, with good sales and good earnings.

The trend toward volatility has scared many investors. If you want to be a successful investor, instead of following the herd, be a contrarian. Perhaps one of the hardest lessons to learn is that when stock prices plunge due to volatility in an industry or the stock market as a whole, this creates some fantastic bargains. A certain amount of courage is needed to think positively when almost everyone else is crying the blues. However, this approach can pay big dividends.

As long as the company you invest in is high quality, even if the market has fallen and may decline further, the company will survive. At some point your bargain stock's price will move up from its undervalued position, and you can smile all the way to the bank as your friends wish that they had been farsighted enough to purchase so-and-so stock when it was so cheap. The smart investor looks at volatility as an opportunity that few take advantage of.

CHAPTER

16

The Scamproof Investor

After the 1987 crash, thousands of small investors hesitated to purchase stocks. Many were cash rich and ripe for picking by scam artists. An estimated $10 billion is lost annually by unwary investors who get talked into great-sounding swindles. Those high-pressure artists will gladly take your money in such diverse investments as gold stocks, oil wells, commodities, futures, options and penny stocks.

☐ RULE 11 ☐

Don't take anyone else's word; investigate before you invest.

INVESTIGATE BEFORE YOU INVEST

When an investor talks to his broker, many times the investor becomes so concerned about how much money can be made that he forgets to ask any questions about the investment. Letting someone else make your investment decisions for you is certainly easier than taking the responsibility yourself; however, this makes you more susceptible to high-pressure investment scam artists.

Let's look at some investment scams to help you recognize the different characteristics involved. Of course, one ingredient that is always there is the investor's greed—a greed that can be so great that it blinds the investor to the scam.

Classic Commodity Half-and-Half Scam

This scam has been used by aggressive brokers who pick any volatile commodity, such as September pork bellies. Starting with a list of perhaps 500 prospective investors, the broker will call half of the investors and tell them to buy. The other half will be told to sell. Needless to say, 250 investors will be impressed with the broker's advice because the pork bellies will either have moved up or down as "predicted."

Then the broker will contact the 250 people who were correctly advised and again divide the group in half, advising 125 to buy and 125 to sell another volatile commodity. Once that commodity either goes up or down, the broker contacts the group that has been twice correctly advised. That group of potential investors by now is extremely impressed with this financial wizard, and many will blindly follow his or her "superior" investment advice. This tactic provides the commodity broker with a steady stream of customers and commissions. The same scam can be adapted by brokers in futures, options and stocks.

How do you protect yourself from such a scam? One way is to investigate the broker before you trust him or her with thousands of your dollars. You can contact your state securities commissioner or local better business bureau to verify that the broker and his or her firm are duly licensed in your state and to learn whether either has been disciplined by any regulatory agency. If the broker has been using underhanded methods to sell securities previously, there's a chance that complaints have been lodged against him or her. You can contact the following associations:

U.S. brokers and brokerage firms

National Association of Securities Dealers (NASD)
Member Services Department
9513 Key West Avenue
Rockville, MD 20850-3389
800-289-9999

(A NASD office is located in each state, usually in the capital. You can call directory assistance for your local NASD office.)

Canadian brokers, brokerage firms and companies

Investment Dealers Association of Canada
121 King Street West, Suite 1600
Toronto, Ontario M5H 3T9
416-364-6133

Commodity brokers, futures brokers and brokerage firms

National Futures Association
200 West Madison Street, Suite 1600
Chicago, IL 60606
312-781-1410
800-621-3570 (800-572-9400 in Illinois)

Following are nine tips that investors will want to observe when considering an investment. Because purchasing stock may involve a lot of money, it can be an expensive lesson if you make a mistake. While the vast majority of brokers and financial analysts are honest, you should be aware that there are unethical salespeople. Misrepresentation of a stock's value and outright fraud do occur.

Scamproofing Your Investments

1. Never buy any investment offered over the telephone without investigating; always ask for written information about the investment so you can review it.
2. Beware of the broker who applies high pressure for you to buy immediately.
3. Check the references of any broker you don't know who tries to sell an investment to you.
4. Be suspicious of "guarantees" of quick or huge profits.
5. Never buy on tips or rumors. It is more prudent to get all the facts first. Besides, it is illegal to buy or sell stock based on "inside information."
6. Recognize that in an investment program, past success does not guarantee success in the future.

7. If you don't understand something in a prospectus or a sales brochure, get advice.
8. Don't speculate unnecessarily. While speculation can be a worthwhile investment tool for knowledgeable, experienced investors who understand the risks involved, for the average investor, speculation is too risky.
9. Be extremely careful with tax-sheltered investments and limited partnerships or any other investment that claims a much higher return than average.

SPOTTING AN INVESTMENT SCAM

Perhaps the best-known and most successful swindler of the twentieth century was Charles A. Ponzi, who emigrated from Rome to the United States in 1903. He has the dubious distinction of being the father of the "get rich quick" scheme. In 1919 Ponzi formed the Securities and Exchange Company (SEC) in Boston.

Ponzi's scam was simple—lend me your money for 45 days, and I will pay back not only your principal but 50 percent interest. The gullible public flooded him with money—almost $10 million. He would pay back the early investors with new investors' money. This strategy worked until July 1920, when Ponzi was bringing in more than $400,000 a day but couldn't repay earlier investors. Ponzi, the ultimate smooth talker, claimed, "The promise of a profit is not larceny, it is merely a promise, and a promise may or may not be kept according to the circumstances."

Almost 70 years after Charles Ponzi's company was shut down in 1920, the Ponzi scheme continues to flourish. Today's copycats create an aura of wealth with swanky offices, fine clothes and expensive cars (perhaps even a plane or helicopter). Potential investors are fed hints and suggestions about a "very profitable venture that is distributing extremely large profits to investors." Gullible and greedy investors still line up today to throw their money into such schemes.

It is ironic that the Securities Act of 1934 created the SEC (Securities and Exchange Commission) to regulate the securities industry. I sure hope it wasn't named in honor of Ponzi's famous company.

Today there is a new emphasis on financial planning, which is one area that abounds with swindlers. According to a recent two-year study by a group of state securities examiners, "The rapid growth of the loosely regulated financial planning industry appears to have had the unintended side effect of paving the way for the swindlers and unscrupulous promoters who pose as financial planners." The study recommended that potential customers inquire about a planner's experience and professional background and request examples of his or her work and references.

Penny-Stock Scams

One area with a tremendous number of scams and frauds is penny stocks, especially pink-sheet stocks. While a few investors get in on the ground floor of a legitimate company and sell the stock for a nice profit after its price rises, most investors are not that fortunate. Penny stocks are risky investments. A typical penny stock is poorly financed with an uncertain future. Because of its low price and relatively small number of shareholders, the stock can easily be manipulated by its underwriter or market maker.

Perhaps one of the most well-known examples is First Jersey Securities. In the brokerage firm's commercials, the chairman would step down from his helicopter and invite investors to "come grow with us." He would then promote the great investment opportunities in penny stocks. (You may have seen this ad a few years ago when it ran during a Super Bowl game.) After years of run-ins with the SEC on the quality of the penny stocks that this brokerage firm sold, it was forced to close, leaving thousands of investors out in the cold.

Last November I read about an investment scam that hooked both sophisticated and unsophisticated investors in the Midwest. Over 700 investors from the Chicago area alone pumped money into National Liquidators Inc. of Columbus, Ohio. The company, which bought liquidated merchandise and sold it to discount stores, gave initial investors a 30 to 40 percent return on their money. Even Dun & Bradstreet gave National Liquidators a good report. However, investors never saw a brochure or statement. Nothing was verified in writing, except the receipt for their investment. The only information they got was by word of mouth.

As with all good frauds, it worked for a while—in this case two or three years before the house of cards came tumbling down. In October 1993 National Liquidators' president, Vance Wolfe, was accused by the SEC of defrauding investors of $43 million. The company shortly was declared in involuntary bankruptcy. Upon investigation it was found that National Liquidators had never registered with the SEC, a violation of federal securities laws. Investors don't expect to see their money again.

Figure 16.1   Deceptive Advertising

- Apple Computer . . . a penny stock? Not any more, but similar opportunities await the informed investor today. Don't miss the next opportunity!

- How to get rich—investing in the penny-stock market—while some investors have lost, find out how others have made fortunes in the penny-stock market.

- The most profitable penny stocks you ever saw—MCI at $.25 and Tandy (Radio Shack) at $.63. These major companies were once penny stocks.

An interesting scam was perpetrated by a teenager. Barry Minkow became a millionaire by promoting his carpet-cleaning company, ZZZZ Best, from nothing to a value of $100 million. (The company no longer exists, and the stock is worthless.) Investors were bilked out of more than $50 million. Many major brokerage firms were promoting the stock, and it is hard to believe that no one checked ZZZZ Best's 10-K and 10-Q forms to discover that the firm actually had very little sales and assets. Worse yet, no one seems to have questioned why a small carpet-cleaning company with hardly any assets should be worth almost $100 million. Many of the people who lost their money foolishly bought the stock at record-high prices, assuming that the stock would move higher.

Advertising Scams

You can even find scams in your mailbox. Recently I received an advertisement with some interesting statements (shown in Figure 16.1).

Let's review those statements. First of all, Apple Computer was never a penny stock—it went public for almost $20 per share. The statement is totally false. In the second example you see typical penny-stock hype. If the firm resorts to such tactics in its advertising, what other tactics does it use to sell stocks? In the final example Tandy and MCI were never penny stocks. The low price that is used in the example comes from the Standard & Poor's stock guide, which adjusts a stock's low price for stock splits. When a stock splits, say two for one, the low price, which may be $5, gets split also into $2.50. Over the years the Standard & Poor's low price for companies such as Tandy and MCI, which have had several stock splits, has become quite small, even though the stock never sold at that price.

Weeding Out the Scams

I learned a long time ago that determining which investments to avoid is a major step in deciding what to buy. Whenever you receive an unsolicited telephone call from a broker who wants to help you make money by investing in a great little company, beware. By asking the following two questions, you can weed out many potential scams:

1. *Where is the stock traded?* If the salesperson says, "the OTC market," ask where specifically. If it's either the pink sheets or the Vancouver Exchange, avoid the stock.
2. *How did the company go public?* If the company was a shell, a blind pool or a self-underwriting, stay away from the stock.

If you are still interested in the stock, ask that you be sent the company's annual report, 10-K and 10-Q so you can analyze them. Don't let the salesperson rush you into investing before you receive this vital information. If the investment is a good one, it will still be there two or three days later when you receive the information and can make an educated decision.

REGULATION IN THE MARKET—THE SEC

Under the federal securities laws, the major responsibility for regulating the conduct of the individuals and companies that buy and sell securities lies with self-regulatory organizations that are governed by the SEC. The self-regulatory organizations, such as the NASD, institute rules to supervise trading and other activities, establish qualifications for professionals in the securities industry, control the behavior of their members and discipline those members who ignore or break its rules.

The SEC's primary objectives are to make sure that the securities markets operate in a fair and orderly manner, to assure that the professionals in the securities industry deal honestly with their customers and to guarantee that corporations make public all the pertinent information an investor needs to make an intelligent investment decision.

Figure 16.2   SEC Regional and District Offices as of March 1994

Source: Securities and Exchange Commission.

The SEC serves as a watchdog to protect against fraud in the sale of securities, illegal sales practices, market manipulation and other violations of investors' trust by brokers and brokerage firms. The SEC can deny registration to securities firms and in some cases may impose sanctions against a firm and/or individual who violates federal securities laws. Abuses include misappropriation of customer funds or securities and manipulation of the market price of a stock.

Despite the protection provided by federal and state securities laws, it is essential that investors know that they have the final responsibility for their own protection. In particular, the SEC can't guarantee the worth of any security. Each investor must make that judgment for himself or herself.

It is a good idea to check the SEC's library to see if any of the individuals connected with an investment have had sanctions imposed against them. Several SEC offices are located across the United States. The map in Figure 16.2 shows the regional and branch offices.

You may also want to read the following excellent publications:

What Every Investor Should Know or *Investing Wisely*
The U.S. Securities and Exchange Commission
450 Fifth Street, NW, Room 3C38
Washington, DC 20549
202-272-3100 (general information)
202-942-7040 (Consumer Affairs)

Investment Swindles: How They Work and How To Avoid Them
The National Futures Association
200 West Madison Street, Suite 1600
Chicago, IL 60606
312-781-1410; 800-621-3570 (800-572-9400 in Illinois)

Investor Alert–How To Protect Your Money from Schemes, Scams, and Frauds
The North American Securities Administration Association, Inc.
One Massachusetts Avenue, NW, Suite 310
Washington, DC 20001
202-737-0900

The vast majority of all investment scams have one similarity—high-pressure telephone sales tactics. If you are offered a deal that's just too good to be true, it probably is. The best way of handling high-pressure, incredible telephone sales offers is to hang up!

CHAPTER

17

Investing Without Using Money

A painless way to test your expertise in buying and selling stocks is to simulate trading without actually investing the money. Simulation gives you the opportunity to gain experience in trading stocks. It allows you to learn from your mistakes without risk. In this chapter you will apply the knowledge that you have learned from this book.

TYPICAL STOCK COMMISSION SCHEDULE

Pages 118, 119 and 120 show lists of both full-service and discount brokers. You can call or write several firms to request their commission schedule. When you read the schedules, you will probably notice variations in the commission fee depending on the trade dollar amount and the minimum commission charge. You can use that information to your advantage when purchasing a stock. If you already know what stock you want to buy, you might as well use the least-expensive brokerage firm.

To figure your total cost of buying and selling stocks, include the brokerage firm's commission fee. The commission becomes an important element in the cost of investing when you realize that it directly affects your profits. It is easy to forget that fact when figuring profits. Many times an investor will look at the price per share for

Figure 17.1   Commission Schedule

Trade Amount	Commission Rates
100 shares	$ 45 minimum (100 × $.03 = $3)
500 shares	$ 45 minimum (500 × $.03 = $15)
1,000 shares	$ 45 minimum (1,000 × $.03 = $30)
2,000 shares	$ 60 (2,000 × $.03 per share)
5,000 shares	$150 (5,000 × $.03 per share)

both buying and selling and figure that the difference is the profit. Unfortunately, commission fees sometimes consume a good portion of the profit. Because brokerage firms have a minimum fee, I recommend purchasing at least 1,000 shares if at all possible.

Usually low-priced stock commission fees are based on so much per share. The cost per share can range from a high of $.08 to a low of $.015. Each brokerage firm has a minimum commission ranging from $25 to $85. The sample in Figure 17.1 shows how a typical commission schedule would be set up for a firm that charges $.03 per share and has a $45 minimum commission fee.

With the schedule you can determine your commission fee. For example, you want to buy 1,000 shares of Winnebago Industries at $6. Your stock price (principal) would be 1,000 × $6 or $6,000. Referring to the commission schedule, you see that 1,000 shares × $.03 per share = $30. This is below the $45 minimum, and therefore you would pay $45. (If you bought 2,000 shares, the commission would be $60.) Adding the $45 minimum commission to your principal of $6,000 gives you a total purchase price of $6,045.

SIMULATING A STOCK TRADE

Any time you purchase a stock you receive a confirmation from your brokerage firm that looks similar to the one in Figure 17.2.

The stock confirmation has the following ten areas of interest:

1. *You bought/you sold* tells how many shares were purchased if the amount is in the "you bought" area or sold if in the "you sold" area.
2. *Security description* gives the name of the stock you traded.

Figure 17.2   Stock Confirmation

In accordance with your instructions, the transaction below is confirmed for your account and risk subject to terms listed on the reverse side. Please refer to your account number when placing orders or making inquiries. Refer to the reverse side for instructions on endorsing and mailing certificates.

You Bought	You Sold	Security Description	Price	Trade Date	Settlement Date
1,000		Winnebago Industries	$6.00	11-15-93	11-22-93

Account Number	Gross Amount	Interest	Commission	Other	Net Amount
123456	$6,000.00		$45.00		$6,045.00

John Smith
1234 Fifth Street
New York, NY 10001

Confirmation—Customer's copy. Retain for tax purposes.

3. *Price* is the cost per share for the stock.
4. *Trade date* shows the date the stock was bought or sold.
5. *Settlement date* specifies the date the payment is due at the brokerage firm if you bought or when the firm will issue a check to you if you sold.
6. *Account number* is the number of your account with the brokerage firm.
7. *Gross amount* is the price per share multiplied by the number of shares.
8. *Commission* shows the amount charged by the brokerage firm to either buy or sell the stock.
9. *Net amount* is the total amount owed the brokerage firm if you bought or owed you if you sold.

Figure 17.3 Company Information

Stock Record

Company Name **Winnebago Industries**
Address **605 West Crystal Lake Road**
City **Forest City** State **IA** Zip **50436**
Telephone Number **515-582-3535**
Exchange **NYSE** Stock Symbol **WGO**
52-Week High **$11.38** 52-Week Low **$5.63**

10. *Name and address* lists your name and address and should be checked for accuracy.

The stock confirmation indicates that on November 15, 1993, you bought 1,000 shares of Winnebago at $6 per share. The gross price is $6,000 plus $45 commission. Therefore you owe the brokerage firm a total of $6,045, which is due at the firm on November 22, 1993.

Stock Record Worksheet

When you simulate a stock buy, you want to include most of this information on your stock record. The blank form in Figure 17.8 provides space for all the vital information for a particular stock investment on one easy-to-read page. The first section includes perti-

Figure 17.4 Buy Transaction

Buy Transaction

Date **11-15-93** Stock Price **$6,000.00**
Number of Shares **1,000** Plus Commission **$45.00**
Price per Share **$6.00** Purchase Price **$6,045.00**
Why did you purchase the stock? **Good sales, good earnings. Low stock price near 52-week low price.**
Stock Price Projection **75-100% in 9 to 12 months.**

Figure 17.5 Sell Transaction

Sell Transaction

Date _____ Stock Price _$ 11,750.00_

Number of Shares _1,000_ Minus Commission _$ 45.00_

Price per Share _$ 11.75_ Amount Received _$ 11,705.00_

Why did you sell the stock? _Met projected profit level in_
13 weeks.

nent information on the company. If you were simulating the purchase of Winnebago, you would fill it in as shown in Figure 17.3.

The "buy transaction" section contains all the important details of the stock purchase. At the bottom of the section you should express your reasons for buying the stock and the price you project the stock will hit. It would look like Figure 17.4.

When you decide that it is time to sell your stock, you would complete the two bottom sections. The "sell transaction" records the money you would receive when you sold the stock. You also want to write your reason for selling the stock at that point. If you decided to sell Winnebago at $12, you would complete this section as shown in Figure 17.5.

The final section helps you to ascertain how well your investment worked for you. Fill in the left-hand column first to determine your profit or loss. Then complete the right-hand column to calculate your percentage of profit or loss. Perhaps the most important part of the simulation is to analyze what you did right and what you did wrong in choosing your stock. The whole idea is to learn from the simulated

Figure 17.6 Profit or Loss Percentage

Profit or Loss Percentage

Amount Received _$ 11,705.00_ Profit or Loss _$ 5,660.00_

Minus Purchase Price _$ 6,045.00_ Divided by Purchase Price _$ 6,045.00_

Profit or Loss _$ 5,660.00_ Percentage Profit or Loss _93%_

What did you learn from this transaction? _If you can make_
almost 100% in 13 weeks, take your profit.

transactions and avoid losing your money. Figure 17.6 shows how you would fill in the "profit or loss percentage" section for Winnebago.

Writing down all the details of your particular investment is a great educational experience. It also makes it easier to review your buy and sell transaction and learn from it.

Stock Price Data Sheet

The downfall of many investors is not following the stock after they have purchased it. They spend the time to analyze stocks to determine their best investment but then get lazy or too busy to follow their investments. Consequently, they miss some great profit opportunities.

☐   **RULE 12**   ☐

Follow your stock price so you do not miss major profit opportunities.

The stock price data worksheet (see the blank worksheet provided in 17.9) makes it easy to follow your investments. You can write down the stock price every day (which I recommend) or every week, depending on how volatile the stock is. The top section includes a little background information on the stock, including the 52-week high and low and the price you paid for the stock. These three figures are important in analyzing when you should sell your stock.

The main body of the worksheet allows you to write down the daily (or weekly) closing price and the fraction it is either up or down. At the end of the week (or month), fill in the difference for that time period. Keeping this record will show how the stock trades and will allow you to easily determine if you should sell the stock. The stock price data sheet shown in Figure 17.7 illustrates what the daily price move on Winnebago may look like.

Figure 17.7   Stock Price Data Sheet on Winnebago

Stock Price Data

52-Week High	Low	Company Name	Date Purchased	Price per Share
11 3/8	5 5/8	Winnebago		# 6.00

Day or Week	Price per Share	Up or Down	Day or Week	Price per Share	Up or Down
1	6.00	unchanged	21		
2	6.88	+7/8 +875	22		
3	7.50	+5/8 +625	23		
4	7.25	-1/4 -250	24		
5	8.13	+7/8 +875	25		
Change	+2 1/8 2,125		Change		
6	7.75	-3/8 -375	26		
7	7.88	+1/8 +125	27		
8	9.50	+1 5/8 +1,625	28		
9	9.25	-1/4 -250	29		
10	10.38	+1 1/8 +1,125	30		
Change	+2 1/4 2,250	10,375	Change		
11	10.50	+1/8 +125	31		
12	11.00	+1/2 +500	32		
13	11.75	+3/4 +750	33		
14			34		
15			35		
Change	+1 3/8 2,000	11,750	Change		
16		Sell	36		
17			37		
18			38		
19			39		
20			40		
Change			Change		

Selling Price: # 11.75

Figure 17.8   Stock Record Worksheet

Stock Record

Company Name _____

Address _____

City _____   State _____   Zip _____

Telephone Number _____

Exchange _____   Stock Symbol_____

52-Week High _____   52-Week Low _____

Buy Transaction

Date _____   Stock Price _____

Number of Shares _____   Plus Commission _____

Price per Share _____   Purchase Price _____

Why did you purchase the stock? _____

_____

Stock Price Projection _____

Sell Transaction

Date _____   Stock Price _____

Number of Shares _____   Minus Commission _____

Price per Share _____   Amount Received _____

Why did you sell the stock? _____

Profit or Loss Percentage

Amount Received _____   Profit or Loss _____

Minus Purchase Price _____   Divided by Purchase Price _____

Profit or Loss _____   Percentage Profit or Loss _____

What did you learn from this transaction? _____

_____

Figure 17.9   Stock Price Data Worksheet

Stock Price Data

52-Week		Company Name	Date Purchased	Price per Share
High	**Low**			

Day or Week	Price per Share	Up or Down	Day or Week	Price per Share	Up or Down
1			21		
2			22		
3			23		
4			24		
5			25		
Change			Change		
6			26		
7			27		
8			28		
9			29		
10			30		
Change			Change		
11			31		
12			32		
13			33		
14			34		
15			35		
Change			Change		
16			36		
17			37		
18			38		
19			39		
20			40		
Change			Change		

Selling Price: _____

CHAPTER

18

How Much Have You Learned?

Winning Big with Bargain Stocks, 2d edition was written to help you become a wiser and more profitable investor. By investing the time to read and analyze this information, you have taken the first step. Applying this knowledge to your future investments will give you a more solid foundation for making smart investment decisions.

This book has covered diverse topics, such as how to find potential investments, how to analyze them, the positive and negative aspects that can affect a stock's profit potential, tips for buying and selling your stock for the best profit, locating the right broker for your needs, how to avoid scams and how the economy can affect the stock market. You have the information; now it is up to you to apply it.

This final chapter offers the opportunity to test just how much you have learned. The questions that follow cover some of the facts you should know. The page number in parentheses indicates where the answer can be found.

Chapter 1: Following Your Investment Dream

What are the 12 rules that make up the CHEAP   (p. 3)
   philosophy?

Why are stocks listed in 1/8s?   (p. 6)

Chapter 5: Analyzing Stocks Easily and Profitably

Chapter 6: Mastering Stocks under $10

GLOSSARY

accounts payable A liability reflected under the "current" section of a balance sheet. It may include the total of amounts due within one year for the purchase of inventory or other direct costs, general overhead expenses and other amounts owed.

ADR American Depositary Receipt is a receipt in the form of a certificate for U.S.-traded securities representing stock in foreign corporations.

annual report The yearly financial statement of a corporation's financial condition. The report shows assets, liabilities and earnings, as well as a description of the company's operations—how it stood at the close of the business year, how it fared in terms of profit and other information of interest to shareholders.

AMEX The American Stock Exchange is ranked second behind the NYSE in most stringent requirements for listing.

asked The lowest price that is acceptable to a seller of a security at a particular time. Price that a potential shareholder would have to pay to buy stock in that security.

asset   Any item of value that is owned by a business, institution or individual.

balance sheet   A condensed financial statement providing a picture of a company's assets, liabilities and capital on a given date.

bear   Someone who believes the market will decline.

bear market   A declining market in stocks usually brought on by anticipation of declining economic activity.

bid   The highest price a prospective buyer is prepared to pay at that specific time for a security. Price that a shareholder would receive if he or she sold the stock.

blue chip stock   Shares of a company known for the quality and wide acceptance of its products or services with a steady record of profit growth and dividend payouts and a high probability of continued growth and future growth.

blue-sky laws   The popular name for laws enacted by various states to protect the public against securities frauds. The term is said to have originated from a judge who asserted that a particular stock had about as much value as a patch of blue sky.

book value   Determined by the total assets of a company, minus liabilities and preferred stock. The sum is divided by the number of outstanding common stock shares.

broker   An individual who acts as an agent in the buying and selling of investments.

bull   Someone who believes the market will rise.

bull market   A rising stock market. Usually lasting at least a few months, bull markets are characterized by large trading volume.

capital gain or capital loss   The profit or loss difference between the purchase and sale price of an investment.

cash flow   An accounting term describing the positive or negative effect on cash generated from operations. It is the net income of a corporation plus amounts charged off for depreciation, depletion, amortization, etc.

certificate   A document proving ownership of a security. It usually is finely engraved with delicate etchings on watermarked paper to discourage forgery.

churning   A practice of overactive trading of customer accounts to generate commission income for the broker rather than to make a profit for the customer.

closely held corporation   Any corporation in which a substantial portion of the voting shares are held by a small number of shareholders.

closing price   Price at which a security trades at the close the day.

collateral   Securities or other assets pledged by a borrower to guarantee repayment of a loan.

commission   The broker's fee for buying or selling a security.

common stock   Securities representing an ownership interest in an incorporated enterprise. Common stockholders have a residual claim on earnings and assets after all debt and preferred stock obligations have been met.

conflict of interest   A situation in which an individual who has control, influence or authority over a company may personally benefit from actions or decisions made by that company.

conglomerate   A corporation that has diversified its operations usually by acquiring enterprises in widely varied industries.

consumer price index (CPI)   Published by the Department of Labor, the index measures the prices of consumer goods and services.

convertible   A bond, preferred share or debenture that may be exchanged by the owner for common stock.

current assets   A company's tangible assets that are held in the form of cash or any other form that could be converted to cash within one year.

current liabilities   A company's debts that are due and payable within one year.

day order   A type of buy or sell order that is valid only for a single trading day.

debenture   A promissory note backed by the general credit of a company and usually not secured by a mortgage or lien on any specific property.

depreciation   A bookkeeping entry. Normally, charges against earnings to write off the cost, less salvage value, of an asset over its estimated useful life.

dilution   A decrease in the percentage of ownership in a corporation to an individual shareholder when more shares are issued to other shareholders.

discount broker   A broker offering only services to buy or sell securities. The commission is cheaper because he or she gives no investment consultation, advice, literature or other support.

discount rate   The interest rate charged by the Federal Reserve System on loans to member banks.

diversification   Spreading investments among different types of investments, companies, industries and risks.

dividends   Payments made by companies to their stockholder, usually from profits.

dollar cost averaging   A system of buying securities at regular intervals with a fixed-dollar amount, rather than purchasing a specific number of shares or units.

Dow   Usually refers to the Dow Jones Industrial Average, the most commonly used stock market index.

downtick A transaction made at a price lower than the previous transaction.

earnings per share The amount of net income earned per share of common stock after payment of dividends to preferred shareholders.

earnings report Also called income statement, this shows a company's earnings or losses over a given period.

effective date The date when a registered offering may be sold to the public.

face value The par value of a bond, printed on the face of the certificate, indicating the amount the issuer promises to pay on maturity.

fiscal year A 12-month business year chosen by an organization for tax and financial reporting. The fiscal year may end at any month.

float Shares of a security available for buying or selling. Shares in the public hands as opposed to closely held.

Forms 10-K and 10-Q Reports filed with the SEC by all listed corporations. The 10-K is an annual report, and the 10-Q is a quarterly report.

fundamental analysis The evaluation of a company by studying its management, financial and competitive positions.

going public Offering securities to the public for the first time.

gross domestic product (GDP) Formerly called the gross national product, the GDP is a measure of a nation's total output. It is the value of goods and services bought and sold, including personal consumption, government purchases, investment in business equipment and the net difference between foreign purchase of American exports and domestic purchase of foreign imports.

growth stock A stock with a record of rapid growth or the potential for rapid growth.

holding company   A corporation that owns the securities of another, in most cases with voting control. A holding company may be formed to manage and control several related companies.

hot issue   A security about to be offered for sale that has generated extreme interest and should trade above the public offering price.

hype   To promote a stock with misleading or inaccurate information.

inactive stock   A stock that trades a very low volume of shares. Many inactive stocks are traded in 10-share units rather than the customary 100-share units.

income statement   A financial statement providing a picture of the company's interim earnings. Income statements report total revenues, costs, expenses and net earnings from operations.

inflation   The economic environment in which prices rise, resulting in a decline in the buying power of the dollar.

inside information   Company affairs that have not been made public. It is illegal to use inside information on, for example, a takeover attempt or greatly changed earnings to buy or sell stock for a profit.

insider   An officer or director of a corporation, anyone who owns 10 percent or more of a company's voting stock or an individual with inside information.

institutional investor   An organization whose primary purpose is to invest its own assets or those held in trust by it for others. It trades in high volumes, receiving discounted commissions for block trading.

interest   The payment a borrower makes to a lender for the use of the lender's money.

investment   Using money to make more money, to gain income or increase capital or both.

investment adviser   An individual who provides financial consultation. The title is used by financial planners, registered investment advisers and securities and insurance salespeople.

investment banker   Another term for an underwriter or any person or firm helping a corporation issue new securities.

investment company   A company whose sole purpose is to earn income by investing the pooled capital of many other investors in other corporations.

IPO   The initial public offering of a stock to the investing public.

issue   Any of a company's securities or the act of distributing such securities.

junk bond   A bond with a speculative rating of BB or lower by Standard & Poor's and Moody's rating systems. The ratings range from AAA (highly unlikely to default) to D (in default).

leverage   The technique of using borrowed funds or special types of securities (warrants, calls) in an attempt to increase the rate of return on investment. While the rate of return using leverage is greater, the risk to the investor is also increased because the principal and specified rate of interest must be repaid.

liabilities   All obligations or debts owed by a corporation.

limit order   An order to buy or sell a security, if it is possible, at a specified price.

liquidation   The process of converting securities or other property into cash.

liquidity   The ease with which an investment can be converted to cash.

listed stock   The stock of a corporation listed on one of the major exchanges. To become listed and maintain that listing, a corporation must meet certain criteria.

load The sales charge assessed against investors in mutual funds, direct participation and other investment programs. The load usually covers sales commissions and all other distribution costs.

manipulation Buying or selling a security for the purpose of creating the false or misleading appearance of active trading. The creation of an artificial price movement, either by or down, to induce the purchase or sale of the security by other investors.

margin Buying securities with a percentage of the purchase price borrowed through the brokerage firm.

market maker A dealer on the Nasdaq exchange who maintains firm bid and offer prices in a particular security by standing ready to buy or sell round lots at publicly quoted prices.

market order Order to buy or sell a security at the best available price.

market price The current or last reported price for which a security traded.

municipal bond Tax-free bonds issued by state and local governments.

NASD National Association of Securities Dealers is a self-regulatory agency for brokers and dealers in the Nasdaq securities business.

Nasdaq National Association of Securities Dealers Automated Quotations system is an information network providing price quotations on securities traded on the system.

net income The profits from company operations. Net income may mean actual income either before or after deducting applicable federal income taxes.

net worth Assets minus liabilities. Total shareholder's equity in a corporation.

new issue The sale of a stock or bond that has not previously been offered by a corporation.

NYSE The New York Stock Exchange is the world's most prestigious investment trading market and has the highest standards for stock listing.

NYSE composite index The composite index of all stocks listed on the New York Stock Exchange, weighted by the number of shares outstanding and reporting the change in value. The index assigns a dollar value to that change to indicate relative movements.

odd lot A stock trade of fewer than 100 shares. Round lots are traded in groups of 100 or multiples of 100 shares.

offer The price at which a security is offered for sale. (Same as asked price.)

open order An order to buy or sell securities that has been given but is not yet concluded. It can be closed in three ways: cancellation, execution or expiration.

option The exclusive right to buy or sell property or securities at a specified price within a specified time. An option usually has a much shorter time period than a warrant.

Over the Counter Securities traded among broker-dealers and not through listings on an exchange. Securities include those of corporations that do not meet the listing criteria of the NYSE or AMEX exchanges, government and municipal debt securities and the securities of many financial service companies (banks, insurance companies, etc.). Name recently changed to Nasdaq.

paper profit or loss An unrealized profit or loss on a security caused by the price either moving upward or downward from the investor's purchase price. Paper profits or losses become real only when the security is sold.

par value The dollar amount assigned to a common share by the company's charter. Par value has little significance as far as the market value of common stock is concerned.

penny stocks Low-priced issues, often highly speculative, selling for less than $1 per share. Often used as a derogatory term. A few penny stocks have grown into exceptionally high-quality companies.

pink sheets A publication listing the bid and asked prices as well as the market makers of Over-the-Counter securities that do not have a stock symbol. Pink-sheet stocks can be very speculative, with large spreads between the bid and asked prices.

portfolio An individual's or institution's securities holdings. A portfolio may contain bonds, preferred stocks and common stocks of various types of enterprises.

preferred stock Like common stock, except usually without voting rights. However, specified dividends are paid to preferred shareholders before dividends are paid on the common shares.

price-earnings ratio A stock's market price divided by earnings per share for a 12-month period. A low PE ratio is considered relatively safe but less likely to increase in value in a bull market. A high PE ratio indicates greater risk and volatility.

primary market The initial market for the distribution of securities. After the initial sale, they are traded in the secondary market.

producer price index Formerly called the wholesale price index, the PPI measures wholesale inflation.

profit taking Selling a stock that has gone up in value since its purchase order to realize the profit. Profit taking is often the cause of a downturn in the market following a period of rising prices.

prospectus The official selling circular that all companies offering new securities for public sale must file with the SEC. The prospectus offers detailed information about the company's financial position, planned use of the new funds and the qualifications of the corporate officers, etc.

proxy A signed authorization by a shareholder allowing someone else to represent him or her and vote his or her shares at the shareholders' meeting.

proxy fight The attempt by a group of shareholders to obtain enough votes to replace a corporation's management or overrule it on specific decisions.

proxy statement The SEC-required statement of information about the items being voted on, which must be given to shareholders when a solicitation for a proxy is mailed.

public offering The sale of securities to the general public.

quotation or quote The highest bid to buy and the lowest offer to sell a security at a specific time. If your broker gives you a quote on a stock as 1½ to 1¾, it means that if you wish to buy stock it would cost you $1.75 per share; however, if you wish to sell stock, you would receive $1.50 per share.

rally A sudden and unexpected increase in market value, either in the stock market as a whole or a particular industry or security.

random walk A theory of market behavior that states that the price of securities cannot be determined but is entirely random.

regional exchanges Stock exchanges that serve distinct regions, such as Philadelphia, Pacific, Boston, Chicago, etc.

registration Before a new security can be offered to the public, the security must be registered under the Securities Act of 1933. The company must disclose pertinent information relating to its operations, securities and management.

reverse split The reduction of the total number of shares outstanding by reissuing shares at a higher par value. Usually bad news for shareholders.

rights The opportunity (at the company's discretion) for shareholders to acquire new stock at a specified price and in relation to the number of shares currently held.

round lot The basic unit in which stocks are traded. For most securities this is 100 shares.

Schedule 13D A Schedule 13D must be filed with the SEC by any person who purchases or acquires 5 percent or more of the securities in any corporation registered with the SEC.

SEC The Securities and Exchange Commission is a federal agency with direct regulatory authority over the securities industry.

secondary market A market in which securities can be bought and sold by the public, following an initial offering.

sell order An order given by a customer to a broker-dealer to liquidate (sell) a security on the market.

shareholders' meeting The annual meeting held by a public company to give shareholders a voice in company actions.

shares outstanding The number of a corporation's shares that are owned by the public (including management) and not held by the corporation in its treasury.

short sale A form of speculation in which the price of a stock is expected to decline. Securities are borrowed and sold and are later bought back at the lower price.

sinking fund Money regularly set aside by a company to redeem its bonds, debentures or preferred stock from time to time as specified in the company's charter.

SIPC Securities Investors Protection Corporation is a government-sponsored, nonprofit organization that insures customer cash and securities on deposit with a member securities firm.

specialist A member of the NYSE who acts as a broker in the execution of orders and as a dealer by transacting for his or her own account. The specialist maintains an orderly market in the stocks for which he or she is registered as a specialist.

speculating Purchasing high-risk, volatile investments with the hope of realizing large returns.

Standard & Poor's Corporation An influential company in the investment area that rates bonds, collects and reports data and computes market indexes.

stock limit order An order to buy or sell a security when its price reaches a certain level.

stock split   Dividing a company's existing stock into more shares and reducing the price per share to improve the marketability of the shares. Also called a forward split.

stop loss order   An order to sell a security if a certain price is reached. Used to protect profit.

stop order   An order to sell at a price below or buy at a price above the current market.

street name   Securities kept in the name of a broker instead of the customer who actually owns the stock. This occurs when the securities have been bought on margin or when the customer wishes the security to be held by the broker.

syndicate   A group of investors who agree to raise capital to purchase the securities of an issuer. Also referred to as an underwriter.

takeover   The acquiring of one company by another.

target company   A company that is the subject of a takeover attempt by another company.

tax loss carryforward   A tax provision allowing losses to be claimed in the years after the loss occurs. Can be used to offset profits so less tax is owed.

tender offer   A public offer to purchase shares of a corporation from existing shareholders. The tender offer specifies a price and time period for the offer.

thin market   Term to describe either a single security or the whole market when there are very few bids to buy or offers to sell.

third market   Trading of stock exchange-listed securities in the Nasdaq market by nonexchange member brokers and all types of investors.

ticker   Instruments that display both the volume and price of security transactions worldwide. Nowadays the display is usually computerized; years ago it was on ticker tape.

tip Advice to buy or sell a stock made on supposedly "inside" information.

trader An individual who buys and sells for his or her own account for short-term profit.

underwriter Usually an investment dealer who agrees to buy all or part of a new-issue security from a company with the expectation that the security can be resold to the public.

unit A minimum amount of common stocks, warrants or other securities that are accepted for trading on an exchange. New-issue stocks may offer a unit composed of various amounts of common stock, warrants or other securities.

uptick A transaction made at a price higher than the preceding transaction.

volatility A measure of price movement in a security, industry or entire market.

volume The number of shares traded by either a specific security or a whole market for a given period of time.

warrant A certificate giving the holder the right to buy securities at a specific price, usually within a particular time period. When a stock's price is higher or expected to be higher than the warrant's specified purchase price, then the warrant has a market value and is frequently traded.

when issued An abbreviation of "when, as and if" issued. Applies to transactions made on a contingent basis, when a security is pending issue and made on the assumption that the issue will occur in the near future.

yield The return on an investment expressed as a percentage of the current price.

INDEX

Let **The CHEAP Investor** Show You How To Be a Smart Investor!
Get Your Free Copy Now!

The

CHEAP

Investor

The Investor's Guide to Quality
Stocks and New Issues under $5 per Share

For more than 13 years, Bill Mathews has been choosing
profitable stocks in **The CHEAP Investor**. Now you can receive
a FREE copy of the latest issue at no obligation!

Here Are Just a Few of **The CHEAP Investor** Superstars!

Company	Recommended Price	High Price	Potential Profit
Arrow Electronics	$3.75	$43.00	1046%
Atari	1.00	12.75	1175
Bank of Texas	.29	3.75	1100
Care Plus	1.00	25.88	2488
Nova Pharmaceuticals	1.63	24.25	1392

You too can make profits like these. For a free sample of **The
CHEAP Investor** and subscription information, call, fax or mail
the lower portion of this order form.
